Why Was This Book Written and How Should You Read It?

In my work, I repeatedly encounter the same recurring pattern among single men everywhere.

There are several things most of them have in common: They have invested heavily in their professional lives — education, work, career — but as a result, they have missed out on their personal lives, placing them as a secondary priority for a while.

They are stuck in the routine of home, work, and studies. They lived for a long time with the fantasy that everything would soon fall into place, that someone special would appear, and they could continue with their routine. However, they eventually realized that things don't happen on their own unless they take action.

Now, when they finally have time for their personal lives, they don't exactly know where to start or how to achieve the things they haven't had until
now, particularly in the romantic aspect. They simply don't have enough experience and insights in this area. Many of them also suffer from
shyness and fear of failure, which prevent them from gaining the necessary experience.

There are both older and younger men who feel stuck in this routine. They want to meet someone but aren't sure how to do it in the best possible way. Dating apps don't really work for them and don't yield satisfying results. The confusion outweighs the understanding in this matter for them.

This book is intended to help them, and any man who wishes, to quickly
gain the necessary experience to reach the same level as men who have always been successful with women and understand them well. To gain
the insights they would have if they had spent many years learning about women.

Do not judge the author without trying the approach. Many things (such as communication methods, reactions, behavioral patterns) may

initially seem illogical, but when you try them and experience them, you will underst
and that these are the things you've been missing all along. You may even enjoy them, and not just you — also the people you communicate with.

I assume you are reading this book not just to enrich your general knowledge, but to use this knowledge or at least parts of it, at least once
or twice in your life. I know you are lazy, and if no one tells you exactly what to do and how to do it, you won't do anything, and the most complicated action you'll take in the coming hours is to turn to the next page. Therefore, the book will include exercises that you will need to do.
 It's a good idea to prepare a notebook now to write down all the exercises and tasks I give you and give yourself feedback on the execution.

The Real Secret to Success with Women — Limited Perspective vs. Correct Perspective

From childhood — in kindergarten, school, and university — we were

taught many things. We learned step by step how to eat and how to walk. We learned history, languages, mathematics, computers, and physics. We learned in sports classes to run, jump, and swim, but no one ever taught us how to communicate with other people and understand them, especially

not with women.

We were not taught anything related to flirting, dating, conversation, or relationships. The ability to captivate another person, especially in an intimate way, was not developed in us.

Sources of information on the subject certainly exist, but how reliable

are they? Teen shows and romantic movies for young people, where the hero pours out his heart, kisses the girl against the sunset, and in the next moment, they're already waking up in the morning. You could have learned how to get a girl into bed from older friends, most of whom, of course,

didn't know more than you, but were convinced they had the winning formula — get her drunk and into bed.

We received information about sex itself from pornographic films starting at the age of 13, and in the absence of other sources, these films remained our best friends for the coming years. In adolescence, no one asks parents because it's not socially acceptable, and at 18, when the pressure starts and you desperately seek answers, you are supposedly already an adult and shouldn't ask parents such questions. Magazines write such nonsense that it's almost sad to read.

Common Misconceptions About Success with Women

Over time, based on information from movies, songs, soap operas, and even grandma's tales, a belief system has developed within us. This system tells us who a man should be and how he should act to win over a woman.

We believe that:

- To succeed with women, you need to look good.
- To succeed with women, you need to have a successful career, money, and luxury.
- To succeed with women, you need to be tall, fit, and muscular.
- A beautiful woman would never be attracted to someone overweight or wearing glasses.
- To succeed with women, you need to have a good sense of humor, be funny and witty.
- To succeed with women, you need to know how to tell interesting stories.
- You need to invest in her to win her over, to work hard for love.
- You have to confess your feelings to her and wait for her to do the same.
- To win over a woman, you need to give her many compliments and show her that you find her attractive.
- Her wishes are law. She must be pleased!

Do any of these statements sound familiar?

If so, you are holding the right book, because these beliefs have nothing to do with success with women. Some of them are even destructive. The beliefs I listed above are blatantly incorrect, but for some reason, society instills them in men from a young age. I won't elaborate on the reasons for this within this book, as that could be a topic for an entire book on its own, but you will certainly receive the best guidance here on how to break free from the vicious cycle of mistaken perceptions.

If you are one of those men who say to themselves, "I can't succeed with women because I'm not good-looking enough or talented enough," you are fooling yourself. If you look around, you will see many men with the same "flaws" (overweight, short, poor, skinny, and unattractive), but they succeed wildly with women! It may go against your perception, but this is the point to stop and think — what exactly do they have that makes them succeed with women? What do they know and do that you don't?

Usually, when an intelligent man sees another man, perhaps a bit "rough" in his behavior, succeeding with women, he tells himself, "You shouldn't behave like that! I can be much better than him. What he's doing is wrong!" Because he is intelligent and used to being smarter than others and always being right, he also believes that his belief system is the most correct, and he acts according to it. It's just a shame that neither his behavior nor his perception leads him anywhere, but instead leaves him empty-handed, while the "rough" guy with the "wrong beliefs" spends an amazing night with a wild cat.

None of us like to admit that we don't know something or that we're not doing our best. We prefer to blame things beyond our control — height (I was born short), looks (my face isn't attractive), money (I wasn't born into a wealthy family).

Let me tell you a secret — any man can succeed with women; he just needs to know how!

What you're missing isn't a nice car, money, or a heart-stopping look. What you're truly missing are skills, the correct perspective, and experience.

At one time, it seemed strange to me that people take courses in entrepreneurship. I didn't understand what there was to learn, and I told myself either you have it, or you don't! In the past, people believed that one is born with the talent to raise children. Today, everyone knows very well that there are many courses on parenting and raising children. Anything can be learned and improved upon.

Learning to succeed with women is just like learning to drive properly, just like taking a course before the SATs, just like studying at a university and gaining experience to understand and succeed in any field in life.

The book you are holding has the potential to shake your worldview and build you a new, more effective perspective that will allow you to

achieve your goals in life quickly and easily, not only in the realm of women.

You Need to Acquire Three Things for Yourself:

- Correct Perspective — Understand what women need, what excites them, how you should behave with them, and what not to do.
- Tools and Skills — What to do? What to say, how to speak, and what to convey? How to pass their tests? How to respond and act with women so that they will want you?
- Experience — Know how to behave in every situation, feel the right timing and dosage for everything, know how to use the right tools, and communicate effectively to achieve your goals.

In this book, I can give you the correct perspective and show you what skills you need to develop, but you will have to gain the experience yourself. You can do it alone, with a friend who reads this book with you, or by joining one of our courses.

Remember: Skills + Perspective + Experience = Success!

Adopt the Attitude That Will Lead You to Success

I have a friend, an ordinary guy with an average job, an apartment in a high-rise building, and a completely normal life. But the women he dates

are the kind of women anyone else would dream of being with. Some are models, and some are businesswomen, but what they all have in common is that they all look amazing and are fun to be around. When I asked him how he managed to connect with these women and interest them, despite being an average guy without much money or striking looks, he told me the following: "I believe I deserve to date the best women, the ones I want. When I meet someone like that, I approach her, talk to her, and we get to know each other. I never try to win her over or impress her; I simply talk to her. If she says something I don't like or behaves in a way I find unacceptable, I tell her that and don't back down just to show her that I accept her as she is and am willing to sacrifice everything just so she'll like me. If I see that she's someone I could be interested in, we exchange phone numbers or make plans to meet again, and we go from there."

I bring up this example to illustrate that success begins with your attitude toward everything you encounter in your life. From your belief about what you deserve and what you don't. From your belief about how people are allowed to treat you and what behavior you will not tolerate under any circumstances. From your approach to every situation and from the position you are in when you make decisions and take action.

In this chapter, we will talk a lot about the principles that will give you the right attitude, which will serve as the foundation for your success with women.

Adopt the Beliefs of a Successful Man

Each of us is a product of our thought process. Our thinking is based on beliefs that we have acquired over time, and we act according to them. Beliefs are the logical rules that reside in our minds and help us process information. We adopted these rules throughout our lives, and today, we believe they are true.

Beliefs drive our behavior. We always act based on what we believe in. We do what we think is right to do and don't do what we think is wrong to do. Based on beliefs, we draw conclusions. For example, I might have a belief that says, "If a woman smiles at me, she wants to impress me," and that's the conclusion I will draw when someone smiles at me. On the other hand, someone else might have a belief that says, "If a woman smiles at me, she wants to gently dismiss me without offending me." People with two different beliefs will interpret the situation completely differently and as a result, behave differently.

Beliefs are divided into two groups:

Supportive Beliefs — Beliefs that allow us to do what we want and act in a way that helps us achieve our goals.

Example: Women enjoy when I approach them and are happy to engage in an interesting conversation with me. A person with such a belief can easily approach a woman and will find it much easier and more comfortable to start a conversation with her.

Limiting Beliefs — Beliefs that prevent us from doing the things we want. We could have done them if we didn't have these beliefs.

For example: "A mall is not a place where you can meet someone." A person with such a belief will never approach anyone in a mall and will not start a conversation with her, even if she is the woman of his dreams. The belief limits him and reduces the possibilities of action in his life.

Based on beliefs, we draw conclusions and choose how to act. As a result of the behavior, we get outcomes. It looks like this:

Beliefs -> Behavior -> Outcomes

In other words, beliefs lead to outcomes in our lives.

Question for thought: How will your life look in 5, 10, or 20 years if you continue to believe what you believe today?

I will give you eight rules and beliefs that will put you in a position from which your actions will lead you to success. According to these beliefs, many men who are wildly successful with women live their lives, and today you will also be exposed to them.

> 1. **I am a man who feels the need to be with a woman, to conquer and seduce her. It is natural and excellent. I have every right to do what I see fit to achieve this.**

Your role as a man is to continue the generation and the human race. To do this, you need a woman. The simplest and most accepted way is to identify the woman who interests you and get to know her. There is no need to hide your natural impulses, as they are completely natural and serve both you and your women. If you are somewhere and see someone you want to meet, you can simply approach her, talk to her, and see if she is ready at this stage in her life to meet someone, and it is perfectly fine to do so.

> 2. **I am one — they are many.**

What would you do when you stop a taxi, inquire about prices, and the driver asks you for a price five times higher than the standard rate? I assume you wouldn't accept his terms, but rather think to yourself, "That's not reasonable," and wait for the next taxi. You have self-respect, and there's no reason to try to convince the driver to take you at the price you want or offer him a bribe. You know there are plenty of taxis that will gladly take you at a reasonable price. For some reason, this is typical behavior for men with women — chasing after "the one" who makes life difficult for a man, not necessarily the most beautiful or intelligent, instead of looking around and by next week already being with someone amazing and fun.

If we make a rough estimate, there are about 3 million women in the country. Around 500,000 of them are in the age range that interests you. About 200,000 of them look average or better according to your taste. About 100,000 of them are smart, intelligent, and fun to talk to and be with. About 30,000 of them live in your area in the country (but with our small country and the capabilities of the internet, this is no longer relevant). About 10,000 of them are available or looking to meet a new man (and I'm making a lot of assumptions here).

So what if things don't work out with one? There are still 9,999 women left!

And if things don't work out with another one, or you decide she's not suitable? There are 9,998 left!

And what if, during your learning process from this book, you fail with another 10 women? There are still 9,988 left!

Do you understand that they are many, and you are one? You will never be able to go through all of them, and there will always be more! There is absolutely no reason to fixate on one woman. Keep your values and demands, and move on.

> 3. **When I talk to a woman, when I flirt with her, I enjoy the challenge and the process.**

Why are we doing all this if not for the enjoyment of communication with women, the challenge, and progressing toward our goals? You enjoy being in the company of a woman and communicating with her. If you feel good and comfortable in her company, only then can she enjoy your company too. If not, you're probably doing something wrong, or you're not suitable for each other for different reasons.

Another point to consider — everything you do, you need to do for enjoyment, because you enjoy doing it. Take the whole subject of flirting

and seduction as a game. It's a game of emotions, excitement. Men tend to attribute a lot of seriousness to the subject and don't understand that for women, all the fun is in the excitement they get from this game. Therefore, from now on, you make this game fun, exciting, and enjoyable for both yourself and the woman. Set aside the aspiration for a result, and start enjoying the game itself. If you're having fun — it means you're doing everything right!

> 4. **Women greatly enjoy receiving attention and signs of interest. This thought gives me confidence every time I see a beautiful woman and approach her.**

Every woman wants love, pampering, understanding, and emotion. Therefore, your sincere smile helps each one understand that you are the one she is looking for. Every woman wants by her side a man who will make her feel like a woman. You have the opportunity to give her this feeling.

5. **Flexibility leads to success. I try different ways until I find the most effective way in every situation.**

Despite the great similarity, each woman is different from another. Each has different values, desires, and behavior patterns. Each has her own approach and way of communicating. If you behave the same way with each one, you will get different results, not necessarily the results you want. Therefore, you need to be flexible and know how to adapt to each situation.

If one way doesn't work, change your approach and continue in a different way until you find the best way to communicate with the woman in front of you at that moment.

Every time you talk or meet with a woman, learn from your successes and mistakes. This will allow you to find new ways to communicate with women. When something goes wrong, or you encounter an obstacle, your flexibility will allow you to change your behavior and find an alternative way.

6. **Everyone can achieve success. Every failure is an opportunity to learn something new and improve for the next time.**

During your learning process, you will fail a lot. Every failure is an incredible experience you acquire. From this experience, you can learn in the best way. If you could succeed immediately, there would be no need to learn something new. When you fail, it is the best time to look at what you did, your mistakes, and learn how to act more effectively next time (how to give proper feedback, read the chapter on positive feedback). Your failures are the steps you climb. Each such step brings you closer and closer to success. If you are not failing, you are probably not learning anything.

7. **Every woman wants sex. Each one to a different degree.**

In our society, there is a tendency to see the man as the primary consumer of sex and the woman as someone who has sex just to satisfy the man's needs and fulfill a duty. Surprisingly, this belief still accompanies many people. You need to understand that both the man and the woman are on the same side of the barricade. Women need sex even more than men. If a man can satisfy himself, such satisfaction is not enough for a woman. A horny woman wants sex so much that she is willing to climb walls. The only difference is that the way she wants to get to sex is often different from the way you want to get to sex. Understand, every woman needs sex and will gladly receive it from the right man.

8. Life is the longest and most wonderful adventure we have, and this adventure we experience only once!

I don't want to explain this statement, and I will leave it for you to understand in your own way. I only want you to understand one thing. Every second, minute, hour, and day that passes is the time of your life. The time that no one will ever give back to you. Therefore, live every moment as if it is the last moment of your life, in which you are ready to devote your all to living the life you want!

I suggest that from time to time, you come back and read these beliefs. Right now, you can already feel a mental shift, look at your life differently, and feel the urge to act and do things. Understanding these simple rules will completely change your attitude and the way you communicate with women.

How to Overcome Fear and Start Acting

Often men come to me and say they've read material on how to succeed with women, but when they tried the theories in practice, they couldn't achieve the desired results. When we continue the conversation, it almost always turns out that the man is trying to cross the bridge before he even approaches it. In this chapter, I will give you what you need to know to avoid a similar trap in your learning process.

To do new things, you need to prepare yourself correctly, lay the foundations, and build the structure upon them.

Before you start looking for new ways to connect with the women in your life, it's important to know the rules and principles. These rules and principles will help you progress efficiently, prevent setbacks, and keep you on track steadily. It's crucial that you understand the mechanisms that can work for or against you and how to stay in control of them.

The Primary Goal — Learning and Improvement

It happens that you approach a woman to get to know her and ask for her phone number, and she brushes you off (if it hasn't happened to you yet because you've never approached, don't worry. You'll soon get to the first exercises, and it will happen a lot). You approach another woman, and it's the same. After several attempts, you feel disappointed, say it's not your day, and in a mood lower than the Dead Sea level, go back home. If this happens to you frequently, this rule is especially for you.

To learn and improve in the field of dating and seduction, you need to set goals. The goals you set for yourself should focus on developing skills, abilities, and competencies, not on achieving results with a specific woman. Instead of approaching with the aim of "getting a phone number," set yourself the goal of "learning how to have an interesting conversation with women and enjoying it." In this way, every time you approach a woman, you won't be focused on her phone number, it won't interest you, and it won't be the goal. You will enjoy the conversation itself, and that's the most important thing. You don't approach to get a phone number, and you won't even ask for it. What's important is that you are learning to develop your communication skills with women, learning something new, noting points for improvement for next time, and drawing more conclusions. Instead of setting the goal to "sleep with a woman," set the goal to "learn to be attractive and show sexuality." In this example too, you focus on the improvements you can make within yourself, not on the outcome with a particular woman.

Such an intention allows you to grow and avoid falling into a feeling of failure. Every failure is not a failure but feedback on what you're doing and an excellent way to know what else you need to improve for next time.

Overcoming Brakes or How to Start Getting Over What Stops You

Brakes are a mechanism that starts to work very strongly in some men the moment they see a woman they find attractive. The guy "brakes," stands still, thinks a lot, runs many possible ideas and scenarios through his mind (how to approach, what to say, and what will happen if...), and does nothing. Does this sound familiar?

While you brake, going in circles, you miss opportunities!

Why does a man think? Because he needs to decide how to act in the best way, he thinks about the things that might interfere, he thinks about the reaction he might get in each case, and he thinks about how he will look in the eyes of the people around him. He tries to cover his ass from all sides without actually doing anything. But let's admit it, these are all excuses. It doesn't really matter what others think of you. They are not your boss and not the ones deciding whether to pay your salary. It doesn't really matter how she reacts. Chances are, half an hour from now, you'll forget what she even looked like. Your life won't actually change because of it! The brake mechanism is one of the biggest enemies of a man who wants to succeed with women.

The Chattering Monkey

Let's look at it from another angle. The one responsible for your brakes is

the "chattering monkey" that lives inside your head. Some people call it the "inner dialogue." It's that small voice that's always talking, talking, talking. We call it the "chattering monkey." It talks about everything you're exposed to. For example, when you're talking to another person, the monkey is in your head, criticizing what's happening. It says, "Nice idea," "What nonsense he's talking," "I agree/disagree," "How didn't I think of that?" It happens all the time, even when you're reading this book. I'll give you 10 seconds to listen to it...

Did you hear it? If you said to yourself, "What chattering monkey? I don't have a monkey in my head. What is he talking about?" then that's the monkey! It's there, talking. The monkey is not you. It has a very central role in our lives. For most people, it's the thing that runs their lives. It shouts, praises, criticizes, sometimes says good things, sometimes bad things. Sometimes it says things that help take a step forward, and sometimes things that hold us back. When we do something new, something unfamiliar, something we have little experience with, something we're doing for the first time, that monkey often interferes.

All personal growth is stepping out of your comfort zone, and the "chattering monkey" wants to keep you inside your comfort zone. It will tell you, "She's too fat, she's not my type, I'll approach the next one. Oh, she's already seen me... but it's not polite! She'll brush me off, she has a boyfriend. She's with her grandma! Take a deep breath first! Again! Well, she's already gone..." The monkey will do anything to interfere, throwing thousands of excuses for why not to do what you want to do. It will explain to you exactly why it won't succeed. It will even make you stop desiring her, and you'll be tempted to believe you don't really want her that much after all.

You don't need to silence this monkey, fight it, or give it bananas. The more you fight it, the more it will interfere with you. For now, just notice that it's there all the time. During the first exercises, notice how it appears and starts throwing its excuses. Say to it, "Thanks for sharing, but I need to do what I want," and do it!

First Steps

The first thing you need to achieve is the ability to talk to women freely and feel comfortable with it.

Chances are, if you're not doing this yet, something is holding you back. These are fears, worries, thoughts, and limiting beliefs.

To succeed, you need to gradually overcome these barriers and start communicating with women comfortably whenever you want to do so. This is the foundation of everything.

As long as you don't do anything, you'll keep yourself out of the field and out of the competition. You can, of course, hope that someone introduces you to a girl, and everything flows like in a Hollywood movie, but that's about as likely as winning the lottery without buying a ticket.

Right now, don't expect results. You're in the learning phase. At this stage, your growth, understanding, and progress are what matter. If you focus on progress rather than just the outcome, you'll get there much faster than you imagined.

Soon I'll give you a series of exercises to help you practice the basics and, at the same time, free you from the fears that are holding you back now.

These exercises have several goals:

1. **To let you experience approaching a woman and even starting to chat with her without any concrete goal.** In other words, the outcome of the communication doesn't matter right now, but the act of communicating itself. Meanwhile, open your eyes and ears and listen to everything that's going on. Write down notes afterward. This is very important!
2. **To let you experience small, unplanned successes.** Your fear stems from the belief that to succeed, you have to be someone special. To get this idea out of your head, I want you to experience small successes with women that aren't based on prior planning but come from a random

and purposeless approach to a woman. This will change your perspective.
3. **To give you a real opportunity to learn about yourself.** Pay attention to what exactly you're doing when you talk to a woman and how she responds to it. Without the pressure of "If I screw up, she'll leave in a second." Your goal is also to mess up, to learn what you're doing wrong.

It's nice to take on a task where there's no way to fail, right? This is what you should learn in the first phase. Do it for at least a few days, and then we'll talk about the next steps.

And One More Important Rule Before You Start Practicing:

The woman you approach doesn't have to be a good match for you in any way. She doesn't have to be your type for you to have a conversation with her, so don't try to be too picky at this stage.

Now go out to the street, the mall, the beach, and do the following exercises. Note that they are built gradually so that in each exercise, you can use what you've already done in the previous exercise.

1. **Identify women who pass by you or near you and say "Hello" with a smile.** Their reaction doesn't matter at all. The exercise is just to say "Hello" so they hear it. Some will answer in a similar way, some will ignore, and some will ask if they know you, and that's perfectly fine. Do it 20 times.
2. **Approach women and ask them the following question: "What is the happiest day of your life?"** Let her answer and feel free to chat with her about it. Do it 10 times.
3. **Approach a woman and say, "I noticed something special about you."** Wait for her to ask what it is, and tell her something you noticed when you looked at her. It could be a compliment, something about her clothes, the way she walks, or anything else you noticed (Hint: you're allowed to make something up if you didn't find anything special). Do it 10 times.
4. **Wherever you are, approach women and talk to the first woman you see about anything that comes to your mind at that moment.** For example, ask her opinion on something, ask if the new clothes you bought suit you, or if perhaps you should have chosen a different color?

Ask what she thinks about artificial tanning? Do this until you feel comfortable talking to a woman, until it becomes a daily and natural thing for you. You will start to notice that the responses you get from women will change, and they will react differently to your approaches than they used to. They may even start flirting back and giving you the eye. You will be very surprised.

After you complete the last exercise, you will no longer need pickup lines. Pickup lines are for men who don't understand women, and for two reasons:

A. **With a pickup line, you hide behind a pre-prepared line.** You're not showing her your true self or what you actually think. How do you expect her to be impressed by you?

B. **Success relies on other elements, some of which aren't verbal at all.**

It doesn't matter what you say to a woman, but how you say it and in what context (or more precisely, how the interaction with her develops). Any strange line, in the context of witty humor and gentle, double-meaning teasing, can interest an average woman. No matter how many lines you've learned, no matter how many techniques you know, it all comes down to your internal state and how you feel during the communication with her.

Remember!

You are doing these exercises not to meet women, but to develop skills, get rid of fears, and feel more confident and comfortable when talking to a woman.

After you do the exercises, take a notebook and write down all your conclusions, achievements, and how you plan to use what you learned from the exercise moving forward.

The Game Approach - She Won't Want to Say No to You!

When you approach someone today, how do you do it? Do you do it in a serious manner?

Most men, when they see an attractive woman, start to feel inner tension and discomfort. Even when they approach her, they put on a mask of seriousness during the introduction, as if they are carrying out an important mission and cannot afford to make any mistakes.

When you approach a woman and start a conversation, is it important for you to succeed in this encounter?

Do you examine yourself and make sure you're doing everything right?

Does this stress you out and make you appear tense?

If the answer to some of these questions is "yes," then you are not enjoying the encounter but rather projecting stress and tension. And if you yourself are not enjoying it, what do you think you'll project to the woman, if not the stress you feel? After all, that's what you are feeling inside during the process.

You will continue to feel and project this as long as you are focused on the outcome of success and on doing everything right.

How do you feel when you are near a tense or stressed person? How is it to talk to them? Is it fun? No!

We always want to distance ourselves from people who are not comfortable with themselves because it makes us feel uncomfortable too.

On the other hand, how do you feel when you are near a relaxed person who speaks and acts lightly?

With such a person, you feel at ease, it's fun to talk to them, and it's easier to open up.

How do you want the woman you are trying to get to know to feel? Clearly, you want her to have fun and feel light with you. You want her to be ready to open up to you and enjoy being around you.

The key to success is the feeling of lightness and playfulness. A sense of lightness and playfulness releases tension and lowers defenses. People feel much freer within a game. When a woman is within a game, she is willing to do many things she wouldn't be willing to do in a serious manner.

In a game, we disconnect from the regular rules of life and switch to the rules of the game. There we can invent the rules ourselves at any given moment.

Why do you think the first kiss and many "forbidden" things at a young age happen specifically within truth or dare games, card games, and other teenage games? Because our impulses demand it, and societal norms and personal morals hold us back. But what is "forbidden" in daily life is allowed as part of a game.

Flirting is a playground. Notice that when a woman flirts with a man, she automatically turns it into a game. Because it's fun! It's enjoyable, it's light. She wants her encounter with him to be something she enjoys, not a stressful business meeting.

Always do everything through play, even if the woman tries to bring you back to the seriousness field—don't go back there. That's where her excuses and objections will be legitimized. Sweep her back to the playground, to lightness and fun.

Building the Game Approach

Notice what questions you ask yourself today when you are communicating with a woman or even before you approach her. If the questions are from the following list, then you're in the seriousness field:

- Am I doing everything right to make her like me?
- What should I say now?
- What should we talk about?
- When can I touch her?
- How do I look?
- Am I doing everything right to see her again?

Questions like these move you to the seriousness field, block you from lightness and play, and make you feel tense and stressed.

You try to do something that you yourself are not enjoying. The woman will feel this immediately. She will recognize that you are not truly in the conversation but are worried about other things that stress you out. She will not enjoy communicating with you in this way and will try to answer you briefly to get rid of you quickly.

With such questions, you are focused on "how to succeed," the importance of your actions, and their correctness, instead of being here and now and enjoying the process. Instead of seeing the woman, you see a walking phone number and think about how to get it. She won't want someone who isn't present, who stands next to her but whose mind is elsewhere or in another time. Instead of managing the conversation you started, you're just thinking about how to finish it and get that desired phone number. You can't manage a conversation like this, and neither of you will enjoy it.

To move to the field of play and lightness, you need to ask yourself the right questions that will focus you on "how you enjoy and spend your time having fun."

Ask yourself the following questions:

- What can I do now that will bring me joy?
- She's mine, I wonder if she realizes it yet?
- I wonder what she's good at?
- What interesting things do I see in her?

- What can I do to test her reaction?
- What emotions can I create in her right now? Can I make her angry?
- What else can I make her feel?
- How can she entertain and make me happy?

These questions focus you on your personal enjoyment.

Enjoy, laugh, do what excites you!

Think about how to have fun, not about how to get to know her!

Even if it doesn't end the way you want, you enjoyed every moment!

Your internal state works for you, which increases your chances of success.

When You Take Her to the Playground, You Set the Rules!

When you are light and playful, you are always positive inside. You can show anger or suspicion, and the woman will also experience those emotions, but she understands that it's part of the game and everything is done in a positive way. She will feel interested, excited, and comfortable with you!

Here is an example of how one of our graduates used the game approach:

I went bar hopping in Jerusalem. The method goes like this: you approach someone and ask for her advice on how to approach another woman, then tease her that she doesn't understand anything about women (which, somehow, they really don't). This way, I don't have the pressure of "I'm hitting on her," she doesn't put up objections, because I'm not hitting on her. There are many opportunities for touch and creating interest, and there's the effect of "Why does he want her and not me, am I not good enough?" In short, I tried it yesterday, it was funny:

Me: "Hey, I need your help for a second."

Her: "Yes..."

Me: "You see the blonde over there at the bar?"

Her: "Yes."

Me: "I kind of want to hit on her, but I need a girl's advice..."

Her: "It's simple. Look, there's even an empty spot next to her. Ask if you can sit down, then ask what she wants to drink."

Me: "What, and that will work?"

Her: "Yes, girls like it when guys invest in them right from the start."

Me: "Wait, are you trying to set me up?"

Her: "No, come on, listen to me" "She'll see right away that you're serious and willing to invest."

Me: "Nah, I don't think you understand women very well."

Her: "No one's better than me, I'm the expert."

Me: "Right, right, just like Verda Raziel."

Her: Confused look

Me: "Listen, if I approach her like this, one of two things will happen: either she'll think, 'Wow, another loser trying to bribe me with a drink to get me drunk so I'll sleep with him,' or 'Cool, another sucker buying me a drink.' Which kind of girl are you?"

Her: "What? No. It's…"

Me: "You know what, I'll try it. Wait here, cross your fingers, and look pretty."

Me: "Hey, don't look. Do you see the curly-haired girl right behind me?"

Blonde: "What?"

Me: "I told you not to look, you'll ruin everything! The one in green."

Blonde: "Yeah, the one with the old-fashioned outfit {Yes, definitely, big cleavage is old-fashioned}. Yeah, what about her?"

Me: "She's my dating coach. She told me to ask if I could buy you a drink."

Blonde: "What?!?"

Me: "So, what are you drinking?"

Blonde: "Look, cutie, I don't know about her, but that's not how it works. Not for me."

Me: "Okay, I'll tell her it didn't work."

Blonde: "Maybe it works, but not on me."

Me: I go back to the second woman.

Her: "So, what did she say?"

Me: "It didn't work at all. What kind of advice do you have? You ruined my chances with her!"

Me: Turning to leave

Her: "Hey, wait."

Me: "You'll have to make it up to me for this."

Her: "Come, I'll buy you a drink."

Me: "No, you didn't understand, you can't hit on me like that!"

Her: "No, no." "I'm not trying to hit on you."

Me: "Okay, don't be red, I'm sure the guys in the corner still haven't noticed." "Come on."

Her: <Starts walking, but then my friend arrives and says they're leaving.>

Me: "Hmm... Okay, give me your phone, and you can make it up to me later."

Her: <Still blushing, hesitating. Looks at my friend, then at me>

Me: Pushing my phone into her hand

Her: Writing

Me: <Letting go of her hand, starting to walk out. After a meter, turning my head back to her> "In the meantime, think of better methods." <Leaves>

In this example, many principles are used that you haven't learned yet. I suggest you revisit this example in the future to see how the guy used principles you will learn later in the book.

Interpretations Leading to Success with Women

Now, I will introduce you to one of the main obstacles that every man faces. This obstacle is in the head of every man, including yours. This obstacle was born in us thanks to the education we received and the environment that shaped our opinions and perceptions of life.

To better explain the subject, I want to present it to you with an example:

You got up this morning, got dressed, and went to work. On your way to work, in the elevator, you encountered a beautiful woman who smiled at you. You can interpret the situation in several ways. You could say to yourself, "She's just trying to be nice, so she's smiling at me," or "She's shy and feels uncomfortable around me, so she's smiling," or interpret it differently and say, "She wants me, she wants to impress me, and that's why she's smiling."

What actually happened was that you and she stood in the elevator, and she smiled at you. How can you know which of the interpretations is true? Unless you've taken a mind-reading course, there is no way for you to know for sure what is really happening here and based on which interpretation you should act. Every person has their own interpretation mechanism. Any situation they encounter in life will be interpreted according to the set of beliefs and opinions they hold. The problem is that if you haven't worked specifically on your beliefs and perceptions, in 95% of the cases (and I'm being optimistic with that number), your interpretations will be "negative towards yourself," or ones that do not push you towards where you dream of going.

If you don't believe that a woman can approach you in the mall, and one day a cute girl comes up to you, asks for help, and starts asking you questions about yourself, you'll likely interpret the situation and say, "There's no way she's interested, she just wants help." Even if she shows you signs of interest and says something like, "Thanks a lot for your help, my friends and I are sitting here at the café, you're welcome to join us," you'll tell yourself, "She's just being nice and wants to reward me," and go on your way. You could have interpreted the situation differently and maybe spent the night with her, but your interpretation prevented you from going there.

Our interpretations are present every moment and are an integral part of our lives. There's nothing wrong with them; they're just there. If we learn to work with them and use them to advance our goals, they can definitely benefit us and change our lives 180 degrees.

Based on the beliefs and opinions we have accumulated over our lives, the interpretation mechanism gives an automatic interpretation to every situation and causes us to act based on that interpretation. For example, when a woman tells us about someone else she met, we can say to ourselves, "She's attracted to me and wants me to be jealous and do something with her already." Alternatively, we could think, "Great, she found someone she likes, and now I have no chance with her."

We never know if the interpretation we just thought of reflects reality or not. But we do know that the interpretation is what runs our lives, the decisions we make, and the actions we take.

You need to train your interpretation mechanism and teach it to work in your favor.

You can always recognize that what you're telling yourself is just an interpretation, and you could have given the situation a different interpretation. Until today, this mechanism was automatic for you; you were constantly interpreting without noticing and thought that this was reality. Now you know you have control over it. From now on, start paying attention to your interpretations in every situation, and before you judge the situation, pause for a moment and think—will this interpretation move you forward? Could you have interpreted the situation differently and, as a result, done something different and achieved different results?

Here comes the important part: you can always choose one interpretation from dozens of possible interpretations. From now on, the interpretation you choose is the "real" interpretation for you, and you will act according to it. This is how we create our reality and live in it. What's even more beautiful is that reality begins to behave according to how we interpreted it to ourselves.

Every situation in life can have a positive interpretation that moves you forward or a negative interpretation that keeps you stuck.

For example: If you see two women sitting at the bar and talking to each other, a negative interpretation would be, "They're probably having an important conversation, and I shouldn't interrupt." If that's your interpretation, you likely won't approach them and will never know what could have come from that encounter. A positive interpretation for you would be, "Here are two women waiting for a man to add some color to their conversation." With that kind of interpretation, you'd probably approach them, join their conversation, and go with the flow.

How to Use the Interpretation Mechanism in Daily Life

From now on, pay attention to how you judge situations in your life, how you can turn your interpretations into positive ones that move you forward. Put every interpretation to the test. Always ask yourself, "If I make decisions and act according to this interpretation, where will I end up?" If the answer you give yourself doesn't seem right, change your interpretation to a different one that could lead you to different outcomes.

While it sounds simple, it requires practice. At first, you'll notice a few situations you could have interpreted differently, but as time goes on, you'll interpret more and more situations positively. This will lead to a significant leap in all areas of your life.

Treasure Hunt – Where to Meet Women?

In the coming days, I suggest you perform an exercise.

Every time you're out of the house, on your way to work, in line at the checkout, during lunch at a restaurant, or on your morning run, look around and count the women you see around you that you would like to meet.

You will discover that women are everywhere you are throughout the day. Perhaps except for the men's restroom.

Each one of them can be met! Each one of them can be interesting and sexy! Each one of them could be attracted to you if you just give her the opportunity.

When you do the exercise, you will realize that throughout the day, there are dozens of women around you that you would like to meet, but you don't. Each one of them that you don't approach is a missed opportunity, lost the moment you decided to give up on her.

For a long time, I dealt exclusively with street encounters, and I can confidently tell you – you can meet women anywhere! All you need is to know how to talk to them and make them attracted to you.

There are places where the percentage of single women coming specifically to meet someone is higher. These are places like clubs, pickup bars, and various pubs. However, these are also the places where meeting someone will be the hardest. In such places, every woman, just by being there, signals to all the men around her that she is an object for meeting. There will be many attempts to approach her throughout the evening, so she has to filter out the unsuitable ones. The competition will be tougher, and her defenses will be stronger so that only the strongest can get through. But once you finish reading this book and practice what you learn, meeting someone in the most competitive place will be an easy task for you.

Compared to pubs and clubs, meeting in any other unexpected place is much more pleasant, spontaneous, and unusual.

How to Approach Her?
- Which side to approach her from?
- From the closest side

(From dialogues in the course "The Art of Seduction")

One of the scariest moments in meeting a woman is the initial stage. This is where the most questions arise, and the question "How do I approach her?" is no exception. Of course, the most important thing is the fact that you approach her, but there are several rules that can make the process more efficient for you, create less resistance, and help the encounter go more smoothly. I will tell you about these rules in the following paragraphs.

Every person has their personal space. When someone invades our personal space, we immediately feel it. When the person is a stranger, we feel uncomfortable with their presence.

The best way to approach is to come from the front and slightly from the side. This way, you only turn your head towards her, but your body continues facing the direction you were previously walking. It looks as if you're about to keep walking at any moment. Such an approach is non-threatening, doesn't block her way, and isn't as intimidating as approaching from behind or directly from the front. Schematically, it would look like this:

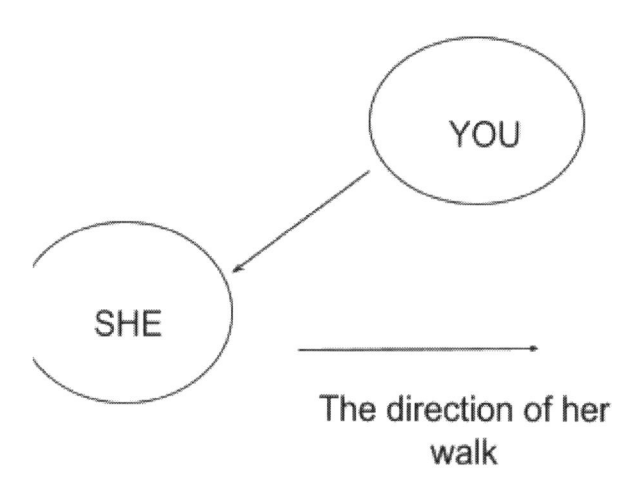

```
         ┌─────────┐
         │   YOU   │
         │         │
         └─────────┘
        ╱
       ╱
  ┌───╳─────┐
  │         │
  │  SHE    │      ─────────────▶
  │         │
  └─────────┘     The direction of her
                         walk
```

If in the situation you find yourself, it's uncomfortable to follow this rule, ignore it. You don't need to circle around, go around buildings, or search for opportunities to approach at the correct angle. It looks ridiculous and will do more harm than good. Follow this rule when it's comfortable and simple to do so. Ignore it if it only complicates the situation.

If you approach her from behind or stop her face-to-face and scare her, there's no harm in it. Despite her slight hesitation, you can always turn the situation into something funny and unique. It happens to me that someone gets startled by an unexpected approach, and I always use it as an opportunity to break the ice, saying something like, "Wow, you're really jumpy! I think you need a few seconds to calm down now," and smile at her gently. Because I use a playful approach, she takes the whole situation with humor; the ice breaks, and we've already had a shared experience and can talk like old friends.

When you're next to her and start talking, don't turn your whole body towards her. Half of your body should remain turned to the side as if you plan to keep walking. The only thing facing her at the beginning of the conversation is your head. This is less intimidating and stressful. When the conversation develops beyond a few sentences, you can then turn your whole body towards her.

When you stand with your whole body facing her, it shows excessive interest. Later, you'll learn that it's okay to show interest only after she has shown her interest in you. You can turn your whole body towards her when you see clear signs that she's interested in you and wants to continue talking to you.

What if She Keeps Walking and Doesn't Answer?

This can happen for two reasons. She decided to ignore you, or she simply didn't hear you.

Never chase after her. If she decides to ignore you, chasing her will only increase her antagonism. Stand where you are and say your line or question again, but louder. When she sees that you're not planning to chase her, she'll realize she was simply being impolite, and almost always, she will step back a few steps to respond to you.

What to Do When You Want to Continue the Conversation While Walking?

When you're walking next to a woman you've just met or approached, always stay half a step ahead of her. Never trail behind her or look like someone chasing her. You are always leading, half a step ahead.

She's Sitting, Should You Stand Next to Her or Sit Down Too?

When you approach a woman who is sitting, try to sit next to her immediately when starting the conversation. Don't stand over her or crouch down beneath her. Don't ask her if you can sit; just grab the nearest chair and sit on it. Don't worry, if she doesn't like it, she'll tell you. Women don't like indecisive men who need permission to do what they want.

Summary
1. Don't approach her directly from behind or in front; approach from an angle.
2. Don't turn your whole body towards her; stand at an angle as if you're about to leave until the conversation starts flowing.
3. If she's sitting, start the conversation and sit next to her

while talking.
4. When you're walking beside her, don't lag half a step behind, but be half a step ahead and lead.

These rules apply everywhere and always – approach non-threateningly, don't open up to her immediately, and join a similar situation to hers to avoid creating distance.

Opening Rules - What to Do When You See Her?

Every interaction has a beginning and an end. The beginning of the interaction is called the opening.

Usually, the first few seconds determine how things will proceed and set the tone for the entire conversation. Therefore, we will give special attention to the beginning of the conversation, so you can start your communication with women in a simple and effective way.

There are three rules that will help you start any conversation easily and in the most effective way for you. Here they are:

1. **The Immediate Approach Rule: Approach Her as Soon as You Spot Her**

The moment you see someone you want to meet, you should approach her without hesitation. The longer you wait, the more fear grows, and you start making excuses and finding reasons not to approach her. You will find countless excuses that reinforce your fears. The longer you wait, the more fear will build up, and eventually, you will find a good reason why you shouldn't approach her. At such a moment, your mind can become your biggest enemy.

The solution is to approach her immediately after spotting her and finding her interesting. No unnecessary thoughts, no prior preparations. See – approach.

If you don't do this, you'll regret it later and won't forgive yourself for not trying.

You're not going to propose to her; you're just going to talk to her a bit and see what kind of person she is.

2. **The First Sentence Rule: Say the First Thing That Comes to Mind Spontaneously**

Without thinking, approach her and say the first thing that comes to your mind.

Don't prepare lines in advance. You'll have a few seconds on your

way to her, and something will pop into your head. It's important to be natural and spontaneous. The most spontaneous sentence is the one you haven't prepared beforehand. The worst thing is a man reciting a line he memorized earlier. Later on, I'll give you the guidelines that will help you come up with your own first line. The first sentence is only meant to attract attention, break the distance, and lay the foundation for communication between you. It has no further significance.
The direction in which things develop will be determined during the conversation and how it unfolds.

There is only one thing that can hinder you here, and that is the fakeness that the girl will sense if you try to trick her by using a line someone else came up with. Believe me, they can sense it as easily as you can smell cigarette smoke.

Prepared lines convey that you're not capable of being yourself and are hiding behind lines you've prepared and are forced to recite.

If you have nothing to say, be honest and say, "Hey, I want to talk to you and ask you a few things, but I actually have nothing to say. You start, and maybe something will come up."

Even if you just say "Hey," because she noticed how quickly you approached her without hesitation, the first impression she will have of you will put you in a much better position than most guys who started with flattery after hesitating.

If you feel a total blackout, just stand there and look her in the eyes without saying a word. Silence is a great way to encourage the girl to start a conversation with you, and you can always use it.

Here are some examples of improvised lines, without any formula, from our course students during exercises:

- "Hey! See that girl over there?"
- "Good choice on the dishes!"
- "Good morning!"
- "I need you to answer a question for me."
- "Your lipstick is a bit out of bounds."
- "What is this style of clothing called?"

All these lines were invented according to the situation in which they were said. Look at your surroundings at that moment and say the first thing that comes to mind about something you see. It would be good if it were something related to the girl.

3. The Feedback Rule: Analyze the Situation Only After the Fact

We were always taught to think before we act. In this case, you must put that rule aside and let your experience and instincts guide you. If you try to analyze what's happening during a conversation with a girl, not only will you lose the thread of the conversation, but you'll also start to stress and think about where you're doing right and where you're going wrong. A stressed man is the last thing a girl wants to get to know. It's better to be relaxed and comfortable so she can also feel relaxed around you. Do the analysis of the situation at home over a cup of coffee. That's the best time to draw conclusions and lessons for the future.

To summarize the opening rules:

A. Approach immediately after spotting the girl.

B. Open the interaction with the first thing that comes to mind.

C. Analyze and think about what happened only after it's over.

Improvising Opening Lines or Crutches for Starting a Conversation

Many men have always sought the ideal opening line – that magical sentence that will sweep the girl off her feet and make the right impression. I will present the issues with pre-prepared opening lines, but at the same time, I'll provide several ways to create effective opening lines.

When you approach a girl, you have two options:

First, present yourself as you are, with all your qualities, fears, doubts, and authenticity. Be your true self. The second option is to step into the shoes of an imaginary character and "act" in front of the girl, presenting qualities that are not genuinely yours. In this case, you might impress her with your "act," but eventually, she will want to meet the real you. I assume that you also want the girl to be excited about you, not just the character you played in that moment.

Pre-prepared opening lines represent the second approach, where you memorize lines. If the girl becomes interested, it's due to the lines you memorized and how they impacted her, not because of your true personality, which you concealed. Eventually, she will want to get to know the real you.

Do you know the feeling when you've prepared a line in advance, and it seems like a good one, but when you actually say it to the girl, it feels artificial and nothing like you at that moment? Women can always sense this kind of bluff, and it turns them off. Instead of seeing a relaxed and genuine guy, they're faced with a man reciting lines as if they were homework to read aloud.

So, What's the Solution for Those Seeking the Ultimate Opening Line?

True, you may not always have something witty or appropriate to say, and you need to have a line ready that you can rely on in such moments. Sometimes it's better to have a line to lean on, like crutches, and do at least something rather than sit on the sidelines and do nothing. If it's hard for you today to come up with a spontaneous opening line, use the rules you'll read about later. Do this until you feel comfortable enough around women to improvise lines and easily start conversations without prior preparation.

I'm not going to give you prepared lines, but I will provide you with rules and guidelines that will help you create a suitable opening line for any situation, so you won't need to memorize pre-prepared lines.

Things to Avoid

Apologies

There's no need to explain to the girl why you approached her, and certainly no need to apologize. An example of a terrible opening line would be something like: "Sorry, I really don't mean to bother you, but I saw you..."

The response you'll likely receive is: "If you don't want to bother me, then don't."

Fake Compliments

Many men tend to give girls compliments just to grab their attention. They believe that if they approach a girl, tell her she's beautiful, and are nice to her, she will have to be nice back and want to get to know them. That's not how it works. Insincere compliments are a cheap manipulation that women detect instantly. Here are some examples of such lines: "Listen, you're absolutely amazing; I have to get to know you right now," or "Listen, your eyes are so beautiful. Where are you from?"

Note that the issue is not the phrasing of the line but the intention behind it. Such a line can definitely work, but it will be much more effective if you say it sincerely and not just to get a positive reaction from her.

Cheesy Pickup Lines

Pickup lines that circulate among groups of guys rarely work on girls, and it's better to come up with something more original. I'm talking about the well-known pickup lines like: "I've been a gardener for 30 years, and I've never seen a flower as beautiful as you" or "Are you an alien? Because I think you fell from the sky." I'm sure you can find more lines of this kind.

Things to Do

I'll give you several ways to create your opening line. You can always choose at least one of them. I suggest that tonight you go out to a café, club, mall, or even just the street in your neighborhood and try them out.

Situational Opener

A line that describes the situation. It comments on the environment and what's happening around it. This type of opener is very gentle, invites interaction, and doesn't put pressure on the girl. It's a casual remark about the situation you throw out next to a girl.

- "The rain today is especially wet."
- "Everyone here seems to be in a hurry to get somewhere."

Opinion Opener

With this type of opener, you ask for her opinion on something. Based on her answer, a conversation can develop if you know how to respond accordingly and expand on the topic you asked about.

- "What do you think about a guy surprising his girlfriend with unexpected gifts but always forgetting her birthday present?"
- "I need a woman's opinion... Do you think it matters if a guy wears a belt or not?"

- "Who do you think enjoys sex more, women or men?"

Behavior Opener

A line that describes, criticizes, or asks something about her behavior. With this type of opener, you can comment on her behavior and even blame her playfully for something.

- "You're acting very provocatively!"
- "You're walking as if you're floating above the street; seems like you're in a great mood."
- "Do you always make so much noise in places like this?"
- "From the way you did that, I can guess what kind of personality you have."

Appearance Opener

A line that describes her and her appearance. You can use it as a compliment, a remark, or a question about her look.

- "You look really beautiful; a little improvement and you could be a model."
- "You're dressed in green. Do you know what that means?"
- "I like your makeup style; do you put a lot of effort into it?"
- "Your shirt is standing out a bit too much here; a small adjustment and it'll be perfect."

Cheeky, Teasing Humor Opener

This type of opener should only be used when you clearly identify that the girl is in a flirtatious mood and will understand that saying this is the beginning of a flirtatious game and is not meant seriously.

- "Did you just pinch my butt?"
- "Stop looking at me with such a seductive gaze! I'm not that kind of guy!"
- "Hmm... you have a horny look in your eyes! It says a lot about you!"
- "I know what you're thinking; your gaze gave you away!"

Direct Opener

With this type of opener, you directly declare your intentions. Here, your goal is to show your confidence, masculinity, and decisiveness.

This type of opener can also be somewhat risky since your intentions are immediately clear and might trigger resistance from the girl. If you learn to use this type, it can be highly effective for you.

You must show that you're taking control of the situation and that she is being swept into a new, exciting, and fun world where you're in charge of everything that will happen.

- "Hey, you caught my attention, and I want to get to know you. I'm [your name]."
- "I want to take you out. Give me your number."
- "You dance really well. I liked it. I want to talk to you a bit. Come sit here."

I hope you now understand that you can create an opening line in any situation; you just need to observe closely and connect what you see to a remark, sentence, or question. You can always ask the girl for help, advice, or an opinion. Social norms that say it's okay to help strangers work in your favor here.

You can practice improvising openers in your notebook. Write down five different new lines for each type of opener. Repeat this every few days, and soon, you'll have no problem improvising an opening line on the spot without having to think about it in advance.

How to Continue the Conversation After the First Line

The first line is meant to grab the woman's attention and bridge the gap of lack of communication between you. The first line is like a rope bridge that you throw from one cliff to the opposite cliff to connect them. When the woman responds, it means she caught the rope on the other side, and now you just need to strengthen it. Once you stabilize it enough, you can walk across and reach her.

There are three ways to continue a conversation after the first line. Each has its own advantages and disadvantages, and each is more suitable for different situations. Here are the details:

A. Continue with the Same Topic

After delivering your first line and receiving a response, you continue developing the topic in the same direction and on the same subject as the first line.

Example:

You: I noticed your bag is made of a special, rare leather. She: Yes, that's right. We have a family business for leather goods. You: So Greenpeace isn't your best friend.

This approach is great when her response to your first line was positive and she willingly engaged with the topic you started.

B. Change the Subject

After the first line, you switch topics and continue the conversation in a completely different direction.

Example:

You: "I noticed your bag is made of a special, rare leather." She: "It's just a regular leather bag." You: "See that couple over there? Do you think they're on their first date?"

You should use this method when her response to your first line isn't enthusiastic and she doesn't show much interest in continuing the conversation. In such cases, there's no point in sticking with a topic that doesn't spark her interest. Instead, switch to something more intriguing, provocative, or challenging.

C. Play a Scene

This approach is intended for extreme situations only, as it stirs up many unexpected emotions, and if you can't control them and steer the conversation back to normal, it could backfire. Use this method when her response to your first line is nonexistent, completely ignoring you, or if her reaction is very cold and dismissive.

What you need to do after an unresponsive first line is to imagine you are now in a situation where she did something embarrassing or said something that others shouldn't know. Once you've decided what the imagined scenario is and what role you will play, loudly accuse her of whatever you came up with. It could be something like, "You were planning to take that necklace without paying!" or a lewd suggestion, "What?? A 200-dollar blowjob? Do you think I'd agree?" or anything else you can think of.

The scene must involve other people. You must shout what you're accusing her of loudly enough for others to notice her. At that moment, she'll become embarrassed, her defenses will fall, and she might even blush and try to justify herself. That's when you need to calm the situation down and start talking to her normally.

Example:

You: "I noticed your bag is made of a special, rare leather." She ignores you. You: "People! She pinched me! I demand compensation!"

The entire scene must be done with a smile and a positive attitude. Even when you're accusing her, she should feel that it's part of the game, not that you're genuinely mad at her. Let her get into character and play along with you in this little game called a scene.

Silences

If, during a conversation or when approaching a woman, you have nothing to say, you can always stay silent and look into her eyes. She will often initiate conversation herself.

You need to know how to use each of these methods to continue the conversation because every situation requires choosing the most appropriate approach.

Never get stuck on the same topic for too long; it becomes boring. The more topics you touch on during the conversation, the more memorable, enjoyable, and multi-faceted your interaction will be, leading to more points of connection between you.

The Story of Matrix - Applying the Principles You've Learned

My friend and I had just returned from a night out during the week, and on the way back, we stopped to fill up on gas.

Another car with two attractive girls pulled up next to us.

They were waiting for someone to come fill up their car, and in the meantime, I made eye contact with the driver and then approached.

Me: "Hey, how much should I fill it for?" I said, smiling. (Improvising an opening line based on the situation)

Her: "What, do you work here?"

Me: "I just love the smell of gasoline while it's being pumped." (Continuing on the same topic)

Her: [Laughs] "There are people who are addicted."

Me: "Tell me, why don't you leave the car when you fill-up the gas?"

Her: "I have a sprained ankle," and she stuck her left leg out the window...

I grabbed her ankle, pulled her sock down a bit, and said, "Whoa... everything's covered in platinum," smiling. Honestly, she had nothing on her ankle; I think she just wanted me to touch her leg. (The playful approach)

Her: "Where were you guys?"

Me: "Do you always get into people's private business?"

Her: [Laughs] "Well..."

Me: [Interrupting her] "If you want to get to know me, I'll need your phone number!" I was about to drive off anyway since I finished filling up before she arrived, and I wanted to leave her wanting more... she gave me her number.

Practice

You've learned a lot of new material—how to approach and start a conversation, how to keep it going, and what attitude to have when communicating with women. Now it's time to practice and experiment with your new knowledge.

The goal of this practice is to gain experience with the new material. The outcomes aren't important at this stage, and there's no reason to expect significant results yet. The only thing that matters is that you try communicating in a new way.

1. Approach 20 women and say "Hello," "Good evening," or "Happy holiday." Make sure to do it continuously and complete the exercise within 5 minutes. This exercise will warm you up and help you open up to communicating with people.

2. Perform this exercise 25 times. Each time, use a different type of opening line, so by the end of the exercise, you will have experimented with each type of opening line five times.

Approach a woman and start a conversation with one of the opening lines you improvise based on the situation. Continue the conversation while maintaining a playful attitude. The most important thing is that you enjoy the interaction. If you're not enjoying it, leave the woman and move on to someone else.

After talking to the woman for a few minutes, you can end the conversation and continue the exercise. If you want, you can ask for her number before parting.

Important Points for Practice

You're not supposed to "hit on" the woman. All you need to do is talk and have fun.

During the conversation, feel free to pause, stop talking, and see if she tries to keep the conversation going.

Once you've completed the entire exercise, open your notebook and write down the conclusions you've reached during the exercise and how you can use what you've learned today next time.

Rules for Creating Interest

One of the first stages in communicating with women is creating interest. This is the stage where you approach her, start talking, and she begins to show interest in you.

Have you ever had situations where a woman you didn't know approached you and explicitly tried to hit on you? She showed interest in you and tried, quite clearly, to get to know you. I hope you have.

Think back to a few of those situations where someone tried to initiate with you. How did you feel at that moment? What did you want to do, and what did you actually do?

When I ask these questions in class, I always get similar answers like:

- I felt a bit uncomfortable.
- I wondered if it was serious or if they were messing with me.
- I acted arrogantly, not sure why.
- I brushed her off, and in hindsight, I don't even know why.
- I felt stuck.
- I was confused, didn't know how to respond.
- I felt threatened and looked for the 'right' way to behave.
- I rejected her.
- I played hard to get and didn't let her get to know me. I put obstacles in her way, unintentionally.

Notice that when a woman explicitly tries to hit on you, you often play hard to get, respond coldly, and eventually just brush her off. Most men automatically dismiss women who approach them. A man simply doesn't feel comfortable when a woman starts with him, especially if he hasn't already shown interest in her. A man wants the woman he's already interested in, not the one forcing herself on him.

What do you think happens with women? The same thing! Women feel the same discomfort, confusion, and desire to brush someone off when someone tries to force themselves on them. Just like men, they automatically dismiss the guy who approaches them if they haven't already shown interest in him.

Now think of another case where a woman approached you, talked to you, asked you something, or requested your help. When it was clear she wasn't interested in you or hitting on you but just exchanging information or asking for help. How did you feel at that moment? What did you want to do, and what did you actually do?

The answers I usually get to this question are:

- I felt fine, enjoyed talking to her.
- I wanted to help her.
- I started to become interested in her.
- At some point, I thought of her as a potential partner.
- I was attracted to her and wanted to keep talking.
- I would have liked to continue getting to know her better.

In this case, when she wasn't explicitly hitting on you, you began to take an interest in her and wanted to keep getting to know her. She wasn't "threatening" you or demanding romantic attention, so you felt much more comfortable around her, enjoyed the interaction, and started to see her as a potential partner.

In the first scenario, the woman revealed her interest right away, which made you feel uncomfortable, and you dismissed her. After all, you weren't interested in her yet.

In the second scenario, you had no idea if she was interested in you or not, but you still started to become interested in her.

If the woman wanted to attract you, all she needed to do was not reveal her interest—at least not until you started to become interested in her. Did you really believe she wasn't interested in you? Of course, she was. But women are very skilled when it comes to relationships. They know how to make you think you're the more interested party. A woman does this by showing a lack of interest until you start pursuing her. She simply lets you feel like you're the one "winning her over" when, in fact, she's already won you over.

I hope you're starting to understand that if we reverse the roles and look at these situations from the woman's perspective, the mechanism is identical to that of a man.

What You Need to Know and How to Act to Get Her Interested

A woman wants the man she's already interested in to approach her. All you need to do is let her become interested in you before you explicitly start pursuing her.

This means you need to talk to her without revealing your interest in her until you recognize that she's interested in you (later, I'll teach you how to recognize when she's becoming interested).

Throughout the entire process, the woman should feel like she's the one winning you over!

Once you see that she's interested in you, you can show that you're starting to be interested in her too, making her feel that her efforts to win you over were not in vain.

I like to compare the rules of creating interest to a card game where each player has a powerful card—the Joker. This card represents one person's interest in the other. The first person to play their Joker loses because they no longer have a strong card, and the power shifts to the player still holding their Joker, who can use it later.

When a man plays his Joker right at the beginning, the woman wins. And a game in which she's already won stops being interesting, exciting, or challenging for her.

Why would a woman want to talk to a man who approaches her with the Joker card on his forehead, shouting from a mile away, "I want you!"? There's no point in playing because the outcome is already clear before the game even begins.

A woman wants a man who holds onto his Joker and makes her play hers first.

Attraction – Activate the Power That Makes Her Want You

To illustrate attraction, I want you to imagine a situation where you're walking down the street or sitting at a bar, and suddenly, you see *her*. She's exactly your type, looks just the way you like, the kind of woman you dream of. Instantly, you start thinking about her and realize you want someone like her to wake up next to you every morning. Now, she's just a few steps away, and you already want her—you can't stop thinking about her. Sounds familiar? Of course! Is it just luck or fate? Maybe, but in truth, it's much more straightforward—the keyword here is *attraction*, and soon you'll understand exactly what I mean.

Maybe it's someone you talked to at school, a bar, or a party, and suddenly you find yourself wanting her. You want her to be with you, you're already thinking about how to impress her and how special she is. She's exactly what you need. On the way home, your thoughts revolve around one thing—her. That woman you barely talked to, yet somehow, she has carved a deep line in your emotions.

Sound familiar? Of course! Is it just luck or fate? Maybe, but in truth, it's much simpler. The keyword here is *attraction*, and soon you'll understand exactly what I mean.

If you try to understand why this happens to you, you might rationalize it like this: she's intelligent, looks exactly how you like, has stunning eyes, has a great sense of humor, and speaks to you as an equal. She's exactly what you need!

Attraction is an emotional response that a man feels toward a woman and a woman feels toward a man. It's that initial infatuation, accompanied by butterflies in the stomach, excitement, and the desire to be physically close to the other person. It's an instinctive and uncontrollable response to external stimuli. The attraction to another person strikes us like lightning on a clear day. Until now, if you've managed to make someone feel attracted to you, it probably happened naturally, without any particular intention or special maneuvers on your part.

Attraction happens instinctively as a response to certain external stimuli.

The same thing happens to a woman. When she is attracted to a guy—she's attracted. She doesn't have a button she can press to stop feeling attracted. She has no control over it. The moment a woman feels attraction toward a man, she tries to get closer to him, to be near him, to win him over.

Remember the story at the beginning? The truth is, her intelligence, sense of humor, and looks weren't necessarily the reasons you started feeling attracted to her. It's just the best explanation you could find for your feelings at that moment. Right now, you can't be sure of the real reasons behind the attraction—you simply feel it.

Our entire lives are based on logic. We're used to thinking that every event has a reason. We always need to explain to ourselves why a certain emotion arises, especially extreme emotions. This is the process of *rationalization*—finding an explanation for a phenomenon that seems logical enough to us.

The things that create attraction often go against the logical reasoning that each of us has. You've noticed that many women say they want a guy who is understanding, considerate, patient, and loving, but they are often actually attracted to "bad boys" and end up dating them.

A woman will want you only if she feels attracted to you. Once she feels that attraction, she'll find a way to explain why she feels it or simply say, "I don't know why, but he just does it for me."

To make a woman interested and excited about you, you need to be skilled at creating attraction. You need to be the man she wants to be attracted to.

Here are some basic rules about attraction:

A. You can't decide to feel attracted to someone. Attraction either happens or it doesn't. It's not a voluntary muscle that we can flex. A woman can't be attracted to someone just because she's asked to be.

B. You can't convince a woman to feel attracted to you. No matter how much you try to convince her to be with you because you're in love with her, she can't just press a button and be into you. It goes beyond logic.

C. We always rationalize attraction and find logical reasons for its presence. Usually, these aren't the real reasons it was created, but they do help us justify its existence.

D. Attraction can be destroyed. A man can make a woman feel attracted to him, and a woman can make a man feel attracted to her. You just need to know how.

Many men today have a clear idea of how they think they should interest a woman. Usually, that idea is far from reality. Men often confuse attraction with likability. Instead of being someone she can be attracted to, he presents himself as someone to be liked and walks around in those shoes. Likability may lead to friendship, but it won't lead to romance.

Let's debunk some myths about attraction.

During the initial interaction and early dates, the man tries to build his image in front of the woman. However, most of the time, he tries to interest her with the wrong things. Instead of using what creates attraction, he tries to make himself likable. A likable man isn't necessarily the man she's attracted to. Feel the difference. I want to show you some things that won't get you anywhere and, in some cases, will be quite destructive, making her lose interest in interacting with you.

A. "Be nice to her, tell her about your feelings, and she'll want you." This is a behavior pattern that leads many women to say, "He's a great guy, and whoever ends up with him will be happy," but they never find themselves being the happy one under the same blanket with him.

B. Chasing after her Trying to win her over again and again in the same way that didn't work the first time—this won't lead anywhere. When you behave in a way that shows her she's the only one for you and you're desperate to win her over, she immediately loses all interest. She understands that you're already hers, and at that moment, you stop being a challenge. Women hate desperation and can smell it from a distance. Chasing after a woman and showing you need her before she's even interested in you is the most destructive thing you can do.

C. Letting her decide for both of you Many men mistakenly think that if the woman makes all the decisions, she'll be the happiest. No, a woman needs a man by her side who will decide for her, who she can lean on and trust his judgment—a man who will take the lead for both of them and take responsibility for decision-making. Whether it's a date, getting to know each other, or in a long-term relationship. If she doesn't like something about his decisions, she'll let him know, but the one who needs to decide and take responsibility is the man. When you let her decide, she starts to feel like she's the man in the relationship and you're the submissive one. She'd rather replace such a man with someone who can play the male role better.

D. Personal tastes and hobbies It's great that you read books, are knowledgeable about geography, and listen to jazz music—these are valuable things that add to your worth. But they aren't what will make her attracted to you. Don't use this information to interest her in the initial stage. She doesn't want to know about your hobbies before she knows you. She'll be happy to discover that you have a rich inner world, but only as an addition to your personality and who you are.

E. Identity and equality Men tend to look for common interests as a reason for getting to know someone or showing interest. "Wow, you do yoga? I did it for a year too. Who was your instructor?"—this does not create attraction! I'm not saying not to talk about it, but the weight you give to these conversations must be very low. Sure, she may be interested in the classes you take and in Cocker Spaniels just like you, but don't forget that she's supposed to be interested in *you*. Don't base the conversation around finding similarities between you. That's not what will make her attracted to you.

F. Compliments Compliments can be divided into two types. Genuine compliments, where the goal is to show you appreciate what you see in her. The second type—compliments with the ulterior motive of impressing her and making her interested in you. Compliments of the second type just don't work, because it's a trick, and women can immediately pick up on the insincerity.

G. Trying to impress Usually, when a man is with a woman he desires, he doesn't behave the same way he does with his friends. Instead, he "plays a role" that, in his mind, will make the woman attracted to him. The woman, of course, realizes that what he's trying to show her and who he really is are two different things, and she immediately catches on to the deception. Trying to impress is trying to be someone you're not. It won't make her attracted to you—it will do the opposite and push her away.

H. Giving Her Too Much Attention - Someone who is always ready to listen to everything she says, hanging on her every word and trying to please her in every way is a great friend, but not someone she will feel attracted to.

What Are the Elements That Create Attraction?

We said that a woman's attraction to a man is an instinctive response to what he projects to her. It's like a button you press that adds to her attraction to you.

You can think of it as a set of buttons within her, and when you press them, she begins to feel attracted to you. You can press these buttons through certain behaviors and particular masculine qualities that you project when interacting with her.

Here is a list of the elements that create attraction:

1. **Confidence, Masculinity, and Control** – What you feel inside and project outward.
2. **Ability to Stir Emotions** – Through words or actions.
3. **Touch** – As a response to pleasant touch, the body releases hormones that create feelings toward the person touching.
4. **Mystery** – Uncertainty about you or about what will happen.
5. **Challenge** – When the path to getting you involves difficulty.
6. **Physical Playfulness** – Physical closeness that includes playful flirting like light shoves, pillow fights, etc.
7. **Attractive Body Language** – Body language that conveys qualities women are attracted to.
8. **Honesty** – When you don't try to be someone you're not. Being true to yourself without trying too hard to impress.
9. **Curiosity** – Making her want to discover more about you.
10. **Teasing** – Witty and playful humor. The ability to playfully provoke her.
11. **Embarrassment** – When a woman feels embarrassed around you, she begins to feel attracted.
12. **Personal Humor** – Humor directed at her that evokes emotion.

Each of these elements contributes to creating attraction towards you. In the following chapters, we will explore these components. Today, you already have all these elements naturally, but each one is active at different levels. Some are more dominant, while others are less so. Some are well-developed, while others are barely there.

It could be that when you're with your friends, you have high self-confidence and know how to make them laugh, but when you're around a woman, your sense of humor and self-confidence vanish. This is a perfect example showing that you have these elements, but they manifest differently in different situations. You need to learn how to strengthen them, especially in the situations where you need them most.

Note! Physical appearance is not included in this list. There are two reasons for this:

A. Physical appearance and natural traits have a minor role in creating attraction. The factor that truly matters is your level of personal grooming and overall presentation. There will be a separate chapter on this topic later. Surely, you've seen an amazing woman with a partner who looks far below average and asked yourself – "What on earth is she doing with him? Doesn't she see how he looks?" Physical appearance isn't the determining factor. Later, you'll better understand why the other factors are more significant in creating attraction.

B. Physical appearance is not something you can easily change. Your body and face cannot be swapped out. You can groom and present what you have well, and this will be addressed in later chapters.

Now that you've learned the structure and general principles of approaching women and understand that you need to know how to create attraction, we can start refining your behavioral patterns and conversation management skills.

In the upcoming chapters, I will teach you how to recognize and pass women's tests, effectively create attraction, and share with you the things every man must know about women.

How to Succeed with Women Without Getting Overwhelmed

The Importance of Emotional Control

There is a critical mistake that most men make when they are with a woman they are interested in. This mistake is the source of many problems and missteps along the way. The mistake is allowing yourself to get too emotional around a woman, which can ruin opportunities due to a lack of self-control.

Many men lose control and become nervous when they see a woman they want to meet. When most men have to call a woman they're interested in, they lose their words and become paralyzed. When a woman tests us, we become nervous and unsure of ourselves.

Remember that there are good emotions—those we enjoy. This article focuses on the emotions that hinder us from achieving what we want and lead us to behave undesirably.

The Only Way to Succeed is to Train Yourself to Control Your Emotions

You need to train yourself not to get too worked up in certain situations for two reasons:

1. When your emotions take control of you, you won't be able to call her, talk to her, or even make the first move.
2. Women are not attracted to men who let their emotions take over and get overly excited about simple things that are just part of life, like talking to a woman.

Women are attracted to men who can control themselves and their emotions because such men cannot be easily controlled, which challenges them. If she can do something to upset you or lower your self-confidence, she can control you. The moment she makes you emotional, you lose your power and transfer it to her.

The First Thing You Need to Understand is How Emotions Work

You need to understand that emotions don't arise because of the situation itself, but because of the high importance you assign to the situation. If you give too much importance to the situation, it will have a strong impact on you. You will fear making a mistake, become tense and uptight, project insecurity, and are likely to fail.

Have you ever wanted to approach a woman, and all you could think about before approaching was how she might say "no" to you, how you might fail, and how it might hurt? Or maybe you were on a date and wanted to kiss her, and all you could imagine was her getting angry and pushing you away!

We let our imagination run wild and create the worst possible scenarios in our minds. Then, we start to freak out because of what we imagined and begin acting irrationally.

Another example: You meet a woman, get her phone number, and call her, but she doesn't answer or call back. What do most guys think? "Maybe she didn't like me; maybe she has a boyfriend; maybe she's trying to avoid me." "Maybe she's with someone else right now..."

The thing is, most of us use our imagination to envision the worst possible outcome. These images make us lose control, distort our common sense, and create excuses not to do what we originally wanted to do.

When It Comes to Women, It's Important to Stop Giving Everything So Much Weight

We need to stop imagining the worst possible outcome. We can never truly know what will happen, what the other person thinks or feels, or how they will react if we do something.

If this happens to you, use these two rules:

1. Imagine the best outcome for yourself—your goal achieved and the fun you will have.
2. Reduce the importance of the situation.

You can reduce the importance of the situation by understanding that everything that happens is part of the learning process. You barely know her. You are learning, improving, and growing. There's no reason your happiness should depend on a specific woman, especially when you're just starting out. What should be important in every situation is not the specific woman but what you learned, what skills you developed, and how you improved. Even if you didn't succeed with a particular woman, you learned a lot, can reflect on it, draw conclusions, and become better equipped to handle similar situations in the future.

For your information, Thomas Edison conducted thousands of "failed" experiments on his way to inventing the light bulb, but he always kept his eye on the goal (not on the failure). Every "failure" moved him one step closer to his goal.

Remember:

When you succeed, you enjoy.
When you "fail," you learn.

Self-Confidence – How to Improve It and Project It Outward

One of the most critical components, if not the most important, of your personal image is self-confidence. Self-confidence reflects your internal state. It allows you to stay calm relaxed, and do things in a way that makes the people around you feel that you are doing the right thing in the best possible way. Self-confidence is part of your charisma—the quality that makes people want to follow you and listen to you. Body language, energy, expression, and success all reflect self-confidence and are equally influenced by it.

But the question arises: how can an average person, who doesn't naturally possess a high level of self-confidence, quickly acquire the beliefs, values, and abilities that a highly confident person has? How can they project self-confidence outward, even if they don't actually have it? How can they feel self-confident, and what should they do to achieve it? How can they move from where they are now to where they want to be?

The Connection Between Body Language and Internal Feelings

Our internal feelings always influence our body language. They are interconnected. Body language is a mirror that consistently reflects internal feelings. The influence works both ways:

- A change in internal feelings leads to a change in body language.
- A change in body language leads to a change in internal feelings.

A human being is a sophisticated system in which everything is interconnected. Every small change affects the entire system. For some reason, sad people can be immediately recognized by their body language, just as you can see that someone is happy without asking them how they feel.

We need a way to help you quickly and easily achieve an initial feeling of self-confidence. Let's consider which is easier for us to control—our body language and behavior, or our internal feelings? I hope you answered, just like me, that it is easier to control your body language and behavior than your internal feelings. It's harder to simply tell yourself, "I'm going to be happy now," and genuinely become happy. But we can certainly stretch, look up, and jump ten times, trying to reach the ceiling with our heads. Since changing one factor leads to a change in the other, we will use this insight to create a feeling of self-confidence. We will change our body language and behavior, as that is easier.

One of the simplest and fastest ways to do this is through imitation. In English, there is an excellent phrase to describe this approach—"Fake It, Till You Make It." You continue to do it to learn the feeling of self-confidence and get used to it.

Guidelines for Projecting Self-Confidence

The following guidelines describe a highly self-confident person's basic principles and actions. To start projecting self-confidence outward, simply make sure to follow them in your daily life.

1. You are calm and not in a rush.
2. Your movements are quick and timely.
3. Your muscles are relaxed, not tense. If you are in an uncomfortable position, change it.
4. You always stand tall. You do not lower your gaze; your head is always slightly raised.
5. You don't smile often, but you smile gently at the right moments.
6. You are dressed neatly and cleanly—all parts of your outfit match in terms of color and fit.
7. You do not miss opportunities—you cannot afford to. When you see a chance, you take it.
8. You speak clearly, with pauses to create suspense and anticipation for your next word.
9. You are not afraid of pauses or silence in conversation. During these moments, you evaluate the other person.
10. You do not backtrack on things you've said, nor do you justify yourself.
11. You have your own opinions and are not influenced by what was just said, but you are willing to listen to and accept others' opinions.
12. You believe that everything will work out as it should. Always!
13. You don't do anything excessively. You know where the fine line between necessity and exaggeration lies.
14. You do not laugh excessively at your own jokes.
15. You are firm in your decisions.
16. You are optimistic and positive about life.
17. You have self-respect.

18. You respect others but do not allow them to use or manipulate you.
19. You know a few steps ahead what you are going to do. If you don't, you always behave as if you do.

I suggest reviewing these guidelines daily or every few days to see how you can incorporate them into your daily life and to discover what works best for you. Always look at what you are already using and what you haven't yet implemented. Each time, choose a few guidelines to work on in the coming days until you have covered them all.

The Fundamental Difference Between a Man Who Fails and a Man Who Succeeds

There are three basic principles applied by men who succeed with women, which we will explore in this chapter.

1. **Don't Try - Do!**

Nothing will happen if you sit at home imagining your ideal girlfriend, and nothing will happen if you go out with your friends to a bar, have drinks, enjoy yourselves, and never approach any woman.

Many men want to meet women, even beautiful and high-quality women, but most of them do nothing about it.

Think for a moment: when was the last time you approached someone? How many times have you seen someone you found really cute but did nothing about it? The responsibility is yours alone—you are responsible for your actions and their outcomes.

In most cases, success lies in places of uncertainty. When you approach someone, you never know what will happen, where it will lead, or what she will say. You can't predict the future, so not approaching a woman because "I don't know what will happen..." is a really poor excuse. Of course, you don't know what will happen—neither does she!

Don't let uncertainty shackle you. Go and take action! You will always find that once you take action, it was easier, more fun, and worth it.

An unsuccessful man often comes from a position of "trying"—a trick he loves so much! When he wants something, he tells himself, "I'll try," and if it doesn't work out, he says, "I tried—it didn't work." Nothing is up to him; he takes no responsibility—it's much more convenient that way. He says things like, "I'll try to meet that girl and invite her home."

A successful person, on the other hand, comes from a position of doing. When he wants something, he says to himself, "I'm going to do it," and then he goes and does it—and guess what the result is?

A guy sitting in a bar with friends, spotting a girl and saying, "I'll go try to meet her," will usually come back empty-handed. Meanwhile, a master (and when I say master, I don't mean he's better, but that he allows himself to have a different mindset) sitting in the same bar with friends, seeing a group of women, says to his friends, "I'm going to bring them over to our table." A few minutes later, the whole group—including the women—is sitting at the same table, laughing together.

It's all about attitude.

When a successful man says, "I'm going to meet that girl and bring her home," I'm sure he has no idea exactly how he's going to do it—he doesn't overthink it, he just does. Why is he confident it will be successful? Because he takes responsibility for the process.

2. Setting Goals

Setting goals is perhaps the most important tool for success. If you still need to set a goal for yourself, how will you know where to go? What are your dreams for yourself, and how do you plan to achieve them?

Not setting goals will simply take you wherever you currently want. You may not want to end up there.

Now let's talk about goals.

Set yourself a big goal, even if it scares you. Only with a big goal can you break it down into smaller goals. Taking a phone number from someone is an example of a small goal—not that I underestimate it, but if your entire ambition is to get a phone number, then what's the point of calling later? Going on a date is a nice goal, but it's also a small goal. Think—what do you really want? What do you dream of? What truly drives you?

Why is all this necessary? Only when you have a big goal will you have a vision. When you work towards that goal or vision, you create intermediate goals along the way.

For example:

Vision: Love -> Find someone I love -> Go out with someone multiple times -> Have a first date -> Get a phone number -> Approach someone.

In this example, love is the vision. The rest of the steps are derived from the vision and form the steps along the way.

Take a few moments and think about your dreams. From there, start setting goals for yourself.

3. Absence of Thought During the Process

When you communicate with a woman in real-time (not over the internet), everything happens "now." You need to understand the situation and respond as quickly as possible—there's no time for overthinking.

If you start thinking and analyzing things during the conversation—why she said this, why she made that gesture, and how to respond appropriately—you will likely just confuse yourself. You will lose the conversation thread and be left with nothing to say (since you were busy thinking instead of engaging in the conversation).

Instead of being involved in your conversation, you'll constantly say, "So, what did you say?" or "Oh yeah... what?" And instead of moving things forward, you'll just think about "how to do it."

When you're involved in the conversation, you must not think and analyze. Do that in a relaxed atmosphere when you get home and sip some hot tea.

The best way to be involved in the process is to let your subconscious lead you. When you drive a car, you don't think about how hard to press the pedal or how many degrees to turn the wheel to take a corner—you just do it.

A successful man doesn't think during his actions. He spots an opportunity and jumps on it. He begins to act immediately, from A to Z.

The Importance of Appearance, Physical Look, and How to Improve Them

I hope by now you've understood that physical appearance has a minor impact on attraction. The main factors influencing attraction are body language, behavior, confidence, internal honesty, and tone of voice. However, when it comes to attire and grooming, there's always room for improvement to project a better image.

Grooming and Shaving One of the first and most important aspects of appearance is shaving and hairstyling. For convenience, I'll make a distinction here:

Shaving – It is recommended to always be clean-shaven. It's much more pleasant to see a clean, smooth-shaven man, especially when it comes to kissing (since you'll be kissing her tonight, right?). If you're a man who loves his beard, that's perfectly fine, but it's crucial to ensure that it's well-kept and aesthetically pleasing.

Should you grow a beard or not? My answer is to do what you like. Some women love men with beards and stubble, and some don't. In most cases, stubble can be prickly, so many prefer a clean-shaven look—but it's your choice.

Haircut – There are thousands of hairstyle options, and each man has his preferred style. Just keep your haircut neat, get it trimmed when needed, and make sure your sideburns are well-kept. If your mom is still cutting your hair, consider going to a professional barber who can give you a proper style.

Clothing Clothing styles are vast, and everyone chooses their own. Some opt for a simple, classic style, while others take it to extremes. It's important to wear clean and pressed clothes. Consistency in style across all elements of your outfit is key.

Colors – Avoid mixing too many colors; 2-3 colors are sufficient. If you choose colorful clothes, make sure there's a consistent tone across your entire look.

Belt – It's very important to wear a belt. A belt speaks to maturity and seriousness. When wearing jeans, go for a thicker belt. When wearing dress pants, a slim belt that matches your pants or shoes will do the job (recommended colors are brown or black).

Socks – Should match the color of your shoes. If you're wearing dress pants and formal black shoes, white sports socks are out of place. Get yourself some black or brown socks instead.

Shoes – Always have polished shoes. Worn-out or torn sneakers should be replaced. A man who invests in his appearance projects seriousness and reliability. When a man is well-groomed and takes care of himself, it shows that he values himself and is willing to invest in his own well-being.

It's important to match clothing styles. Athletic wear pairs well with sporty clothing and sneakers, while dress attire—such as dress pants and a button-down shirt—goes well with formal shoes. A man who shows up at a club in dress pants, a button-down shirt, and blue sneakers certainly looks odd.

Another point worth mentioning is the watch. A watch is one of the characteristics of a serious, successful man. There comes a time when one must part ways with the plastic watch they got in middle school and switch to a sophisticated, stylish analog watch. In the business world, a watch can even make or break important deals (as silly as it may sound, a quality watch conveys status and a refusal to compromise on excellence). For those who dislike wearing watches, there's no need to force it, but if you do wear one, avoid knock-offs that look cheap.

A Little Something from the World In the world of seduction, there's a concept called "Peacocking," derived from the word "peacock." It means dressing in an extravagant and unique way to attract attention from those around you. This concept is inspired by biological research, which suggests that animals like peacocks spread their feathers to attract a mate. Scientists concluded that it's not the appearance of the tail that attracts the female, but the fact that the peacock manages to survive despite its cumbersome tail, which should theoretically have led to its extinction. The tail makes the peacock awkward, yet it still survives, demonstrating resilience and endurance to the females, creating strong attraction.

The practical application of this method is to wear at least one unique item to attract attention. This gives a woman a reason to start a conversation with you, and over time, you'll notice that women will comment on those unique pieces of clothing—those women are attracted to you, and it's crucial to take advantage of that!

The more uniquely you dress, the more attention you'll draw from those around you. Use this principle wisely to create as many interactions as possible with your surroundings. There are those who apply the theory and dress in unique ways but fail to leverage the interest to start conversations, making them seem "weird" to others. Therefore, be careful with excessive use of unique attire unless you plan to act accordingly.

Additionally, people who dress in very unique ways are exposed to many remarks and insinuations from those around them. The ability to handle these remarks contributes to your experience in interacting with people. Women understand that individuals who dress this way are exposed to comments from their surroundings but manage to overcome them—an element that further enhances attraction.

Examples of Small Clothing Items: A unique hat (cowboy or similar), a colorful tie, necklaces with unique pendants, rings, bracelets. At more advanced levels, people show up fully costumed—for example, dressed as cowboys or ship captains.

It's important to note that I don't recommend overdoing this approach, but it can certainly be a fun experience.

How to Captivate Her in Conversation: Talk to Her in a Way that Draws Her In

What happens if you're just a nice guy? Someone who constantly makes her feel like she's on cloud nine and always happy?

You'll be her best friend, but she'll end up sleeping with the bad boy you don't even know exists.

A woman is attracted to a man because of how she feels when she's around him. It's not about what he says, how he looks, or how much money he has—it's about the emotions he makes her feel!

Attraction defies logic; it's driven entirely by emotion. The key in your communication with women is not what you say, but the kind of emotions you evoke in her. It's important that these emotions are diverse—both positive and negative. I'll elaborate on this later, but to help you understand this better, think about why women are attracted to "bad boys." It's because they evoke emotions that other men don't. Women are surrounded all day by guys who flatter them, compliment them every two minutes, and try to please them and make them feel good. It makes them want to vomit. So, when someone comes along who stirs new, unique feelings in them, they get hooked, because they can't get those emotions anywhere else.

No woman says, "Mom, I brought a jerk home." They're not looking for jerks—they're looking for men who can make them feel a range of emotions, including negative ones, because it's unique to them. Most of these guys are "bad boys" simply because the rest don't have the guts to do it. They don't understand that she needs it and are afraid that if they make her feel something negative, they'll lose her.

Remember: A woman doesn't need to *like* you to feel *attracted* to you.

If you give her the full spectrum of emotions, every feeling in the dose she craves, she'll be addicted to you like a drug!

When talking to a woman and trying to create interest, you don't need to be logical—at least, not all the time. A conversation with a woman doesn't need to be interesting in terms of content; it needs to be emotional. Content is only important as a framework for continuing the conversation. An emotional conversation transcends any specific topic. It consists of unexpected reactions, out-of-place statements, and breaking every logical rule in the conversation. Emotional conversation lacks facts. It has opinions, beliefs, assumptions, descriptions, metaphors, accusations, tests, judgments, evaluations, and compliments. Such a conversation evokes feelings of affection, anger, calmness, nervousness, love, hate, pleasure, agreement, resistance, suspicion—all within a single interaction!

It doesn't matter what you say. What really matters is the emotions you create.

Think back to conversations with women that didn't go well—what kind of emotion did you create in them? How did you make them feel? It's likely that you can't recall any positive emotion in those conversations because they were dry and dull. On the other hand, think about the conversations that flowed and were fun—what emotions accompanied those interactions? How did she feel when she was in that conversation with you?

Most men try to *convince* a woman rather than *evoke* emotion in her.

How to Revitalize the Conversation with Emotion

Men often speak in a monotone because most of the topics they discuss daily are informative, meant only to convey information.

If you watch two women having a conversation, you'll see a discussion full of emotions. In such conversations, there's excitement over every little topic—whether it's their nephew's success in swimming class or a new brand from Castro. The conversation will be filled with "Wow!", "How did that happen?", "I can't believe it?!", "That's outrageous!", "It's so beautiful!", and other emotional reactions women find in everything.

Men get excited and find satisfaction primarily from new information and achievements. Women, on the other hand, get excited and find satisfaction from emotions and experiences. A woman needs emotion in her life.

Breathe life into your conversations with women and fill them with emotions. Get angry with her, agree, disagree, be suspicious, get excited, accuse. Create opposing emotions during the conversation, and she will thank you for it by the end.

Do everything playfully. Outwardly, you can show anger or suspicion—she will feel and experience that emotion—but at the same time, she understands it's part of the game, part of the flirtation. That makes her feel interested, excited, and comfortable with you. When you do this, don't forget the playful approach I mentioned earlier in this book. This is exactly the time to incorporate it.

One of our students in the course studied acting, and he said that on stage, you have to show emotions in an exaggerated way. When you express an emotion on stage in a real, life-like manner, the audience simply doesn't feel it—the feeling isn't conveyed strongly enough. Therefore, actors learn to exaggerate the emotion they are portraying. Think of telenovelas: all the emotions there are expressed in an exaggerated manner, not like they are in real life, because only that way can you truly feel them. You should also feel like an actor on stage when talking to a woman.

When you speak to a woman and want to create an emotional response in her, feel the emotion inside and express it outwardly with a sentence. Do it slightly more exaggerated than you would in everyday life with those close to you.

You need to direct the emotion towards the woman—only then can you evoke a strong emotional reaction in her. If you direct the emotion towards the waitress who served you food, you will come across as an "emotional" guy, someone who gets worked up over every little thing, rather than a man who evokes emotions in others. So don't do that—you need to stir emotions in the woman, not in the waitress.

I can't demonstrate in writing exactly how to convey emotion in a sentence, but I'll do my best to describe it in the clearest way possible. Here are some examples of emotions and the sentences you should use to convey those emotions:

Anger - "Never do that again! It's simply disrespectful to me, to you, and to what's happening."

Calmness - "Look at this; there's something about it that radiates peace."

Disinterest - "Yeah... sure... maybe..."

Appreciation - "I really appreciate you doing that for me, thank you."

Hate - "How can you even think that? I can't stand it!"

Pleasure - "Your touch feels really nice; just do it a little lower."

Suspicion - "Was that you who called me 50 times last night from a blocked number?"

Happiness - "I'm so happy to see you! I missed your daily hug!"

Surprise - "You did that? I really didn't expect you to do something like that!"

Accusation - "How could you call me in the middle of the night?! I was sleeping! You have such a terrible memory; because of you... and you're even lying!"

Agreement - "Alright, let's do it. I like the idea too."

Resistance - "We're not going to do that; it's not right for me."

This is a list of the different emotions you need to incorporate into your conversations. You don't have to use all of them in a single conversation, but you must switch between 3-4 different emotions during a conversation with a woman.

When you talk to women, always listen to what they say and respond in a way that evokes an emotion in them. This is what differentiates a monotonous conversation from one that turns into an exciting experience.

How to Captivate Her in Conversation: Talk to Her in a Way that Draws Her In

What happens if you're just a nice guy? Someone who constantly makes her feel like she's on cloud nine and always happy?

You'll be her best friend, but she'll end up sleeping with the bad boy you don't even know exists.

A woman is attracted to a man because of how she feels when she's around him. It's not about what he says, how he looks, or how much money he has—it's about the emotions he makes her feel!

Attraction defies logic; it's driven entirely by emotion. The key in your communication with women is not what you say, but the kind of emotions you evoke in her. It's important that these emotions are diverse—both positive and negative. I'll elaborate on this later, but to help you understand this better, think about why women are attracted to "bad boys." It's because they evoke emotions that other men don't. Women are surrounded all day by guys who flatter them, compliment them every two minutes, and try to please them and make them feel good. It makes them want to vomit. So, when someone comes along who stirs new, unique feelings in them, they get hooked, because they can't get those emotions anywhere else.

No woman says, "Mom, I brought a jerk home." They're not looking for jerks—they're looking for men who can make them feel a range of emotions, including negative ones, because it's unique to them. Most of these guys are "bad boys" simply because the rest don't have the guts to do it. They don't understand that she needs it and are afraid that if they make her feel something negative, they'll lose her.

Remember: A woman doesn't need to *like* you to feel *attracted* to you.

If you give her the full spectrum of emotions, every feeling in the dose she craves, she'll be addicted to you like a drug!

When talking to a woman and trying to create interest, you don't need to be logical—at least, not all the time. A conversation with a woman doesn't need to be interesting in terms of content; it needs to be emotional. Content is only important as a framework for continuing the conversation. An emotional conversation transcends any specific topic. It consists of unexpected reactions, out-of-place statements, and breaking every logical rule in the conversation. Emotional conversation lacks facts. It has opinions, beliefs, assumptions, descriptions, metaphors, accusations, tests, judgments, evaluations, and compliments. Such a conversation evokes feelings of affection, anger, calmness, nervousness, love, hate, pleasure, agreement, resistance, suspicion—all within a single interaction!

It doesn't matter what you say. What really matters is the emotions you create.

Think back to conversations with women that didn't go well—what kind of emotion did you create in them? How did you make them feel? It's likely that you can't recall any positive emotion in those conversations because they were dry and dull. On the other hand, think about the conversations that flowed and were fun—what emotions accompanied those interactions? How did she feel when she was in that conversation with you?

Most men try to *convince* a woman rather than *evoke* emotion in her.

Structure of Communication and Proper Timing for a Successful Interaction

The initial communication with a woman during an encounter can be divided into three stages: the beginning, the middle, and the end.

Beginning - The first few seconds of communication, which include eye contact, initial words, and creating a first emotional impression (interest, curiosity, challenge, etc.).

Middle - The conversation itself, where both of you are engaged and enjoying the interaction. The peak excitement of the conversation is in this stage.

End - When topics run out, and nothing new comes up to talk about. The conversation stops being exciting, the level of interest declines, and you start searching for what to say next.

Never end a conversation at the point of decline or emptiness, as that will be the impression you leave on the woman when you part ways. The taste left after the conversation is the taste of the last few moments. Don't let the conversation die out. As soon as you feel even a hint that the conversation is about to decline, that's the time to either end it or reignite it.

End the conversation as close as possible to its peak so that the feeling the woman remembers is one of excitement. If you sense the conversation is fading, revive it with emotion! Say something provocative, change the subject, shift the conversation 180 degrees, and when it reaches a new high, end it.

End it at the most unexpected moment, to leave her wanting more. I will elaborate more on ways to end a conversation later in the chapter on encounters.

If the woman starts to lose interest in the conversation, it means you stopped speaking with emotion!

How to Refresh a Stalled Conversation

Many times, a conversation can reach its limit—topics run out, and it seems like an awkward silence is about to set in.

This can happen when the woman hasn't given you something to grab onto and continue with, you're not in a creative mood, or you've run out of everything you initially planned to say. Perhaps you feel there's a need to add more emotion to the interaction before it fades completely, but you don't know how to do it. The fact is, you're stuck.

Here are some phrases that can help reignite the spark in such interactions.

These are provocative phrases. Their goal is to make the woman feel as though she's being tested. The structure is very simple, and you can create endless phrases like these yourself: take something factual, often related to her appearance, and derive an unrelated conclusion (you can add a generalization if needed). It is not advisable to use more than one such phrase per conversation

The following examples will clarify the principle to the end:

"It will be written in 'LaIsha' that a girl who speaks rudely to a man wants to have sex with him immediately!"

"A woman who wears tight clothes loves to seduce men herself."

"If a man drinks a lot of beer, his belly grows. If a woman drinks a lot of beer, her chest grows."

"I read in some women's magazine that a girl who looks directly into the eyes of the person she's talking to loves to be on top during sex."

"In the 'LaIsha' newspaper, they wrote that girls with loose hair are either witches or prefer to have sex in crowded places!"

"They say that a girl who doesn't scratch or bite in bed is a slut."

"If you can pass a paper between a girl's teeth, it means she gets aroused easily."

"I saw a program yesterday where they said that by the way a girl walks, you can tell if she's a virgin or not."

"By how close to her palm a girl holds a cigarette, you can tell if she's hot in bed or not."
Be careful when using these sentences. They can provoke unexpected reactions.

Humor – Does It Create Attraction?

I want to talk to you about humor. The idea came to me after encountering several guys in our course who decided they can't succeed with women simply because they lack a sense of humor.

Let's put aside the fact that they haven't done anything to develop such a sense of humor, like reading great books on the subject or learning how to tell good jokes.

Most men believe that humor will make a woman attracted to them and want them, but it simply doesn't work that way. Humor is a wonderful thing, and its contribution to initial attraction and relationships in general is significant, but humor alone won't make a woman feel attracted to you or want to jump into bed with you.

Men try very hard to show off their sense of humor around women, and soon they turn into just their good friend. A well-developed sense of humor might make women want to spend more time with you and be around you, but it won't make them consider you a potential partner. Soon, you'll become the "court jester," getting a lot of female attention but not understanding why they aren't attracted to you.

Men try to make women laugh to get in their good graces, investing time and effort into thinking about how to make her laugh, hoping that she'll feel attracted and fall for them. Many men wait for approval from the woman and ask themselves, "Did she like what I just said?" If she laughs, they immediately think she's into them. I've come across many stories from men who said, "The date was great; we laughed the entire time, but now she won't answer my calls."

The biggest problem is that men try to impress women using humor. They have this idea in their head that if they're funny, she'll like them for it. So they try to be funny, try to impress, and it starts to look desperate and fake—and by the end of the day, they go home alone.

What Kind of Humor Creates Attraction?

Let's make a distinction: there's general humor, those stories and jokes about anything in the world that aren't directly related to the woman with you, which make her smile and laugh. This kind of humor makes her feel comfortable, happy, like she found a safe place where she can laugh—just like a good friend!

The second kind of humor is personal humor, which works on the same principles but is directed specifically at the woman you're with. The idea is that the stories, jokes, or teasing are aimed at her!

When you're with a woman, tease her a bit. The point here isn't to put her down or hurt her! That's not the goal. A comment like "You're fat" or "You're ugly" will do exactly the opposite and push her away. Find something trivial like "that scarf of yours" and make fun of it. If you're on a date and she does something silly, laugh at her, don't hold back. One of my favorite things is to joke that women don't understand anything about relationships or sex—it usually gets a lot of reactions.

You need to treat her like she's your little sister. You're not scared of her; you can always joke at her expense, just like you do with your friends. Don't give her special treatment just because she's pretty or because you want her.

At this point, I want you to know there are different types of humor, and you don't need to try too hard to be funny. Later, I'll teach you how to develop and use witty humor that will make women want to flirt with you just from hearing you.

Eye Contact Games - Captivate Her Without Words

Eye contact games are another powerful tool for creating strong emotions. When two people look into each other's eyes, an emotional tension forms between them, making it an excellent way to make a woman feel something special around you.

I'll teach you about eye contact games through a story that took place about two years ago. It was a small experiment that a friend and I conducted on the invisible signals that men and women send each other when there's minimal attraction and interest. These are the same interest signals we talked about in the previous chapter.

I should remind you that these signals and messages are transmitted subconsciously, not as a deliberate action. For example, if we ask a woman what she just did—if she noticed what she did when she looked at that handsome guy who just walked in—she would usually answer that she did nothing. But we know very well that she made a few almost imperceptible gestures, threw a few special glances, and did a few other small things she wasn't even aware of. If men knew how to notice these subtle yet crucial signals that women send them, both sides would experience fewer disappointments.

We prepared to go out to a bar and see firsthand how this whole thing happens.

We chose a nice bar whose location or name I won't mention, but it doesn't matter because the same thing would have happened anywhere else.

It All Starts at the Entrance

Your entrance is one of the most important and challenging moments. It might even be the most crucial moment of the game, where the first impression is made and people decide how they'll perceive you going forward.

I walk in slowly, not rushing. No unnecessary movements, no hasty gestures. Complete calm. For those who don't know, in every place like this, there are groups of women, single women, and even those who came with someone but are still looking for their catch for the night. Even if they just came to relax and have a good time, the goal always exists in the subconscious, and every guy who walks in is examined carefully.

Women Need to Know You Noticed Them

The moment I walked in, a few glances immediately turned my way. The rest would notice later. It's very important for women to know that I noticed them. If they don't see that I'm open to any kind of interaction, they'll immediately cross me off their list. So, I have to give a tiny bit of attention to each one who looked at me. Already here, I'm showing openness and creating an initial communication channel that will help me later if I decide to approach one of them.

I walked in, not rushing to find an empty spot, not searching for the waitresses who immediately start pestering generously, not hurrying to get anywhere. I simply stop. I stop in place and slowly scan all the glances directed at me. I hold each gaze for a second, smiling slightly. Usually, they immediately look away, but I know that I won't even count to three before she raises her eyes again to see if I'm still looking at her. The secret is not to look away first—it creates slight embarrassment on the other side. It's embarrassment mixed with a kind of happiness that I noticed her, that I acknowledged her existence.

After each one received a fraction of my attention, I can sit down. I know they'll follow me with their eyes until I sit down—there's no chance they won't want to know where I ended up. The game is about to continue. We head in and sit at a table near one of the walls.

When we entered, the place wasn't full yet. We arrived quite early to ensure ourselves a good viewing spot. We placed our order, and a few minutes later, a cute waitress brought us our drinks and food. As time passed, the place began to fill up, and we paused our conversation to focus on what was happening around us.

If you move your gaze from one wall to the opposite one, there will always be a few glances directed at you. I immediately caught two who were playing with me according to all the rules of subtle sexual signals. The rules of the game are simple. Most guys don't know them and don't know how to respond to them in any way.

So What Are the Rules of the Game?

First, you never look away first. The natural reaction when two gazes meet is to look away. No! Most men look away first, allowing the woman to feel in control, and are immediately disqualified in her eyes. I never do that. I always hold the gaze just a bit longer than usual. She always looks away first. An interesting fact is that the one who looks away first is also the one who feels embarrassed. The one who feels embarrassed loses their power in that moment and looks for a quick way out of the situation, while also accepting the superiority of the one who caused the embarrassment. I prefer to be the one who embarrasses, not the one who is embarrassed. I love it when a woman blushes around me, feels flattered, and looks away. It creates a feeling within her, and I'm the source of it. Women are addicted to emotions and get hooked on those who can evoke a wide range of emotions in them—from negative to positive—each emotion according to the need.

But let's return to the rules and continue to understand what's happening. There's another very important rule. If she's interested in you, within about 45 seconds she'll look at you again to see if you're still looking at her. And you will be looking at her! That's it—from that moment, you could say she's yours. Within a few minutes, you can freely approach her and talk; she'll be happy and cooperate. If you don't approach immediately, she'll keep glancing at you throughout the evening. But if you don't do anything, you're disqualified.

NEXT. You're not suitable, you don't have the guts, you didn't use the opportunity she gave you. There will be someone else who will do the job better, and she'll accept him because he doesn't hesitate and plays the game she wants to play.

I need to make a slight disclaimer about what I've written so far. Women can be in different situations, different moods, and accordingly have different goals for that hour, that evening, or that stage in their life. I'm talking about those who are currently searching—those who always leave an option open for someone to suddenly appear. Someone good enough for her, captivating, exciting, giving her security. And that's most women. End of disclaimer.

Women's Tests – Pass Them Successfully and Don't Fall Into the Trap

Women have a filtering mechanism to determine if a man will make it to a relationship or even sex. It's no secret that many men approach an attractive woman, but only a few succeed. The role of the woman is to filter, to choose the man most suitable for her. The man's role is to be active, to pass the filter and win her over—in simple terms, to be the man who gets chosen.

A woman needs a way to evaluate the men who approach her and decide on each one. The best candidates will pass her filtering process. We call this mechanism "women's tests."

This mechanism is active from the very first moment of introduction and continues until she either has sex with the man or decides he isn't right for her and dismisses him completely.

Women's Tests – A Sign You're on the Right Path

Women's tests are not a bad thing. On the contrary, they show that she sees you as an option and is already interested in you to some degree. She just needs to confirm that you are truly a good match. If she wasn't interested, she wouldn't test you at all, as she would have already decided you aren't suitable. So, if you encounter an obstacle that a woman puts in your path, know you're on the right track—it's simply a test you need to pass.

There are two types of women's tests: verbal and non-verbal.

- **Verbal tests** – Related to your communication, where she tests the meaning behind your words and your responses to her statements.
- **Non-verbal tests** – Related to your actions or inactions. What actions you take and what actions you avoid.

Non-verbal Tests

In this type of test, the woman checks if the man does what's needed to move towards intimacy with her. Simply put, is he making progress?

These tests are more relevant after the initial meeting, during the first date and subsequent dates. It's here that she can see if the man takes initiative and moves things forward, or if everything will depend on her again. However, even during the introduction phase, she can already tell what kind of man he is based on his behavior.

These tests can be broken down into three subcategories:

A. Does He Touch Me?

Does the man create physical closeness, or does he stay strictly in the verbal realm? If everything remains verbal and physical closeness isn't established, there likely won't be any progress. The man moves from the category of "potential partner" to "just a friend."

B. Does He Try to Arouse Me?

Beyond physical touch, does he try to create arousal? Arousal is the next step after the initial touch, which the man should aim for with the woman.

C. Does He Take the Opportunity to Get Intimate When I Give It to Him?

When the woman is ready, the man needs to be prepared to take her and use the opportunity she gives him. No woman wants to wait too long. Women also want sex and want to move beyond just talking. Often, a woman goes out with a man on a first, second, and third date, and she's just waiting for something to happen! But the man doesn't make a move. She gives him signals, but he doesn't notice them. He doesn't see that she's been ready for a while. Eventually, her patience runs out, she gets frustrated, and she leaves him.

These three points can be summarized simply: the man must always keep things progressing. The woman shouldn't have to wait until he is "ready." If she is ready to move towards intimacy faster than the man, she will disqualify him and find someone who can do the job right.

Verbal Tests

Verbal tests occur in the following way: she asks a question or makes a statement and watches how you respond. She's testing what answer you give and the meaning of your reaction beyond just the words. I'll break down the meaning for you in the following points.

1. Confidence and Knowing What You Deserve

"You probably just want to sleep with me," she says, and the typical response from the man is to express how important it is for him to get to know her personality and appreciate her as a person. He doesn't really mean it; he doesn't actually give her personality the importance he pretends to. He just wants to make a good impression and hide what's written all over his face.

This is a typical example of this kind of test. You made an impression that you were approaching her with one goal, but suddenly you changed your stance and presented a different one.

In this test, the woman is checking whether you stick to your position or if you retreat at the first obstacle and change your mind.

Typical questions for this type of test are:

"Are you already inviting me over?"

"Do you think I'll agree?"

The only correct answer to these questions is "Yes." Never back down or try to hide your motives.

If you ask for her number and she says:

"I'd prefer you give me yours."

If you agree, it means you've changed your position. You came to get her number, so why are you backing down from your goal and agreeing to other terms?

The only correct response here is, "I came to get your number. I'm not going to leave mine and put the responsibility for contacting each other on you. That's my role."

Tests like these are designed to see if you hold your ground or if you break and suddenly change your stance, start mumbling things like "but... I think it's better... you see..." and try to justify yourself. That's not masculine! If you suddenly change your stance and try to look good, it probably means you never truly believed in your previous position. She's also testing whether you allow others to step on you or if you stand your ground.

A woman doesn't want a pushover. Always stick to your stance, no matter how bad it might seem. Changing your stance suddenly, searching for nice answers, and justifying yourself is the worst thing you can do around a woman.

Let's look at another example:

Her: "I think you're not in my league." (She's testing your worth and whether you'll let her step on you.)

Such comments from the woman border on arrogance and condescension. This is the time to take her down a notch and think if you really want someone like her.

You: "You know, when you talk, your eyebrows move in a really funny way." (You turn her criticism back on her instead of letting it target you, like she intended.)

Another, more subtle response: "That's okay, I already know what can be improved in you for us to be in the same league."

Here, you're implying that she's in a lower league.

2. The Bragging Test and How Successful You Are With Women

Under this category, I'll include two types of tests that are very closely related.

The first test checks if you have any experience with women at all and if other women want you, or if you're the kind of guy no one wants.

Questions in this test are of the type:

"How many women have you been with?"

A great answer would be one that gives her a certain impression of you without providing exact details.

"I've been with different women who I found attractive. I'm still on good terms with some of them."

A man's value rises the more women want him. However, his value drops when he brags about his women. So, on one hand, you need to show that you're desirable to women, but on the other, don't provide specific details about them.

Any question that asks for details about other women is meant to test you for bragging. This is the second type of test.

Questions that test you in this regard are like:

"Are you seeing anyone else?"

"Tell me about the last woman you were with."

This test is to see if she can feel comfortable around you, knowing you won't talk about her to anyone if something happens between you two. If you brag about other women, you're likely to brag about her too.

For such questions, you should never give an exact answer, because you never know what she's really looking for or what answer she expects. Does she want to know you're experienced, or does she want to be sure you're not a player?

Her: "How many women have you been with?"

You: "I never talk about my past relationships. Whatever happened between us stays between us." (This shows discretion.) Another witty response: "What, was I supposed to count them?"

3. What Role Are You Fit For?

Women understand very well that they don't have to "give" to everyone to get different things from different men. Some guys are suitable for hanging out, some are good for lifting spirits, some are there to help in tough times, and some are willing to spend money on her. Most will settle for a kiss on the cheek, while some will move mountains after a kiss on the lips. If you haven't yet reached the type of relationship you want with her, there's no reason to do things for her that aren't aligned with what you want from the relationship.

Remember, if you want to get to intimacy with her, there's no need to go on outings, help her with shopping, or be her personal driver. Once you start doing these things, that will be your role in her life. Your role is defined by your actions.

When she asks you to do something, ask yourself whether you're in the status you want to be in (for example, her boyfriend) and whether it's appropriate for that status to do what she's asking (like going to the movies together). If the answer to either of these questions is "no," then there's no reason to do what she's asking.

Once you start doing something that defines your role, you've locked yourself into that role.

The Best Way to Pass Women's Tests

The best way to deal with these tests is to make the woman feel like she's being tested herself, right when she tries to test you. If you understand how they do it, you can always do the exact same thing in response to her test. For you, it could be any statement or question that signals to her that she is now being tested, and you are evaluating her worth.

Here are some examples:

Her: "How old are you?"

You: "Are you still stuck on age?"

Her: "How many women have you been with?"

You: "We just met, and you're already interested in my sex life?"

Her: "Do you hit on everyone like this?"

You: "Are you putting yourself at the same level as everyone else?"

Summary

It's important to understand that these are the main categories of tests. There are many other tests you will need to learn to pass. Any question she asks that makes you wonder what the best answer might be is a test for you. Whenever you return home after an outing or a date where you encountered a test you didn't know how to handle, do some self-reflection. Write down a few possible answers you could have given in that situation, so the next time you encounter a similar test, you will be prepared and won't be caught off guard.

When you face one of these tests, don't blame the women for testing you, and don't try to catch them in the act. Most of them are unaware of this behavior and don't even realize they're doing it. Just use your new knowledge the next time you face a test.

This was just a brief introduction to get you acquainted with the topic. In our courses, I ask students to practice these types of tests extensively, as well as others they might encounter. The goal is to develop creativity and learn to respond in a witty and attractive way.

Choose the Right Answer: How to Respond to Her Questions?

This chapter will complete your understanding of women's tests and give you more interesting ways to confront them. One of the most fundamental skills needed for success with women is the ability to understand verbal and non-verbal communication. Men are used to answering questions in a "detail, explain, and clarify" manner, often aiming to "be brief and to the point." It's exactly how we were taught from elementary school onwards—providing all necessary information concisely. This habit is excellent, but only in the right settings.

Have you ever had a conversation with a woman who would give you straightforward, concise answers to every question? After every response, you'd have to think of a new topic to try to keep the conversation going? That's exactly what I'm talking about. If she had answered in a more nuanced way, shared an experience, or responded in a way that raised more questions, the conversation would have flowed better.

When she asks you a question, and you give her all the details right away, leaving nothing else to ask, you kill the conversation. You don't leave anything open to develop, and you wrap up the topic completely so there's no point in continuing. If a woman asks, "Where do you work?" you could have an interesting, emotionally engaging conversation about that for five minutes. But if you just answer, "I work at a bank as a clerk," you kill the conversation.

Remember! Emotions in conversation are very important to women. When you shut down a topic, you also kill the emotions that could have been created around it. When there's no emotion, there's no attraction. The conversation simply becomes a tiresome job interview.

The average man doesn't create any emotion or interest during a conversation; he just exchanges information with his partner. Men tend to be very informational, while women, on the other hand, communicate through emotions. When two people have a conversation consisting only of questions and answers, they both go home thinking about how dry the conversation was. In these kinds of conversations, no curiosity or anticipation is created. She doesn't have to make an effort; everything is handed to her on a silver platter. The conversation isn't an experience, nor is it exciting. There's no mystery, and she's left with no interest in the guy. She simply moves on to the next one.

Another thing to remember: When you answer her questions directly, you're playing by her rules. She sets up the tests, and you try your best to pass them. She asks questions hoping you'll interest her and excite her, but instead, you're searching for the "right," short, and concise answer.

The Best Ways to Answer Her Questions and Create Attraction:

- **Don't Answer Directly or Change the Subject** – When she asks a question, and you don't answer or change the topic, it suddenly creates intrigue. There's something left unsaid, something mysterious. Curiosity arises, and it excites her to try and get the answer you didn't give. If the question is truly important to her, she'll try to pry it out of you, and her curiosity will only grow.
- **Let Her Guess** – Instead of answering her question, say, "Guess. You have three tries." Turn her curiosity into a game, making her work to find the correct answer. You're playing on her desire to show she can figure things out herself.
- **Set a Condition** – Simply tell her, "I'll answer you, but you have to do something small for me first." With this method, you're making a deal: she'll get her answer, but she has to do something for you in return. For example, you could ask her to sing a song, share an experience she's never told anyone, or give you a massage.
- **Give a Partial Answer** – When answering her question, don't give all the details. Leave some parts vague or hidden. This way, she'll feel like you've answered, but there's still a strong curiosity about the missing pieces. She'll know there's more to discover, and the topic will come up again later. Here, too, her interest and excitement are strong.
- **Add a Mysterious Element** – You can answer any question but add a mysterious twist. Provide information that isn't straightforward. For example:
Question: "Where do you work?" **Answer:** "I have a formal job and an informal one." Or, "I work at a bank, but I'm planning to move to something much better."
When she starts digging (and she will), you can say something like, "Let's leave that for now; let's talk about you."
- **Create Emotion** – When she asks a question, you can create emotion by complimenting her for the question: "Great question, I like that you're asking me things like this," or accuse her playfully: "What's with all the questions? We're here to have fun, and you're turning it into a job interview!" Or, "You don't know? How is it possible that someone your age doesn't know this?"
- **Answer with Humor or Give a Ridiculous Answer** – Your answer doesn't directly address her question, and she should understand it's not serious.
Question: "How many women have you been with?"

Answer: "Two concussions and three times clinically dead. I forget a lot of things."
Question: "Where do you work?" **Answer:** "I work in sanitation—taking out trash from the beach."

You must keep a balance here and not turn paranoid about every question during the conversation. There are questions you can simply answer directly, like questions about your age or name. Adopt a rule for yourself: in any conversation, answer every third or fourth question directly, and for the others, use one of the methods you learned here.

Why Do Women Say "No" and Try to Brush You Off?

One of the things that a man dreads, and even causes him to stop himself from approaching a woman, is the possibility of hearing a "no." Automatically, the man starts asking himself, "What's wrong with me?", "What did I do wrong?", "Why did she say no?" By "no," I mean any way she tries to brush you off, not necessarily the word itself. It could be "I don't want to talk" or even complete disregard.

So before you judge yourself, it's important to understand why women say "no." Here are seven reasons why the answer "no" doesn't mean there's something wrong with you, and what's really behind it.

A woman might say "no" for one or more of the following reasons:

1. **It's a Game** – For them, it's a game! Their fun is in feeling desired and being pursued. A woman presents challenges to her man, which he must overcome to win her over. She doesn't want to give herself easily or agree to what the man suggests on the first try. She wants to feel like a magical princess whom the good prince overcame all obstacles to rescue. She doesn't necessarily do this on purpose; it's an internal mechanism that makes her feel like she's worth the effort.
2. **"No" Creates Tension** – Women thrive on excitement and emotions. We've already discussed how women need this kind of feeling and the tension that arises in a situation for their enjoyment. The moment a woman says "no" to the man standing in front of her, tension is automatically created in that situation.
3. **A Simple Filtering Mechanism** – Every woman learned a trick during her adolescence: When a man approaches her, she says "no," and he immediately gives up and leaves. He doesn't really try to get what he wants, and then she understands that he didn't really want it in the first place. A woman doesn't want to be just one of many; she wants to be the one that the man truly desires.
Besides that, imagine an average or above-average woman. Let's say she gets approached ten times a day. It's impossible for her to stand and talk to every guy who wants to meet her for 10-15 minutes. That would take her nearly two hours every day! She has to filter. So she immediately says "no." Anyone who isn't serious, who is shy or afraid, immediately leaves her alone. She can't give every guy who wants to meet her all the time in the world—

she has her own life.
4. **"No" Gives Her Security** – The woman needs to be sure that the man wants her and won't discard her in the future. Imagine applying to a prestigious academic institution and being rejected because of your average grades. You go back, work hard, improve everything, and there's just one test left to get accepted—but then you give up. This shows a lack of seriousness. That's where the woman's "no" comes in; if the man truly wants her, he'll get her despite the first "no," and this way, she'll be sure that she's important to him, that he's already invested in her, and won't just throw her away at the first opportunity.
5. **Women Are Afraid** – Imagine for a moment that you're walking down the street, and suddenly a hot, sexy woman approaches you, tries to get to know you, and asks for your phone number. What would your reaction be? You'd probably be in shock, think it's a joke, not know what to do, and not believe she's serious. You'd want to be sure she isn't making fun of you and that you won't look foolish if you agree right away. For women, it's even worse. They are very afraid of looking bad, of being laughed at. They don't believe you're serious, and they're even more worried about what you'll think of them and whether they're behaving properly in that situation.
6. **Beliefs** – Every woman has her own beliefs. Some believe that a mall, a street, or a clothing store is not the right place to meet men. That men who approach them in the street aren't the kind of men they should be getting to know. In such a case, if you approached her on the street, she would automatically say "no." It's her behavior pattern, and to break it, you need to know how to act correctly in that situation, identify her beliefs, neutralize them, and be consistent even after the first "no."
7. **She's Not in the Mood** – Something happened in her life, and she currently prefers to be alone, without anyone interfering with her thoughts or diverting them from what's on her mind. She just doesn't feel like talking to anyone, no matter how they look or behave. Maybe she's simply in a hurry and not willing to be delayed in any way.

Remember, even when a woman brushes you off, never take it personally. It's not personal against you—she doesn't even know you. She doesn't know you well enough to decide if she wants you or not. It was an automatic reaction; she probably just didn't like the way you did it. If you had approached differently, her response might have been different. Give yourself feedback and take it as a point to improve your skills for the next time.

Never let a woman's words bring your mood down. You must stay positive all the time! That's the key to your success.

How to Overcome the "I Have a Boyfriend" Obstacle

Surely you've experienced this before: you approach a woman, start talking, and at some point, she says, "I have a boyfriend." This could happen right after your first line or when you ask for her number. What's interesting is, you didn't even ask if she had someone, but she decided to tell you anyway.

There can be three different reasons for her saying this:

1. **She's Not Interested** – She simply wants to brush you off, hoping that telling you she has a boyfriend will make you back off. It's her excuse to not continue the conversation or any connection with you. This might happen when you show your interest before creating any attraction or sparking her interest in you.
2. **It's a Test** – A test she might not even be fully aware of, but some women do this intentionally. She's testing you, seeing who you are and how willing you are to invest in winning her over. Women have found this to be an easy way to brush off men who approach them. After all, they can't give five to ten minutes to every guy who wants to talk to them, so they need to filter. They say, "I have a boyfriend," and anyone who isn't confident enough or isn't genuinely interested vanishes. This tells her that you may not be confident or interested enough, and she's not going to be interested in you either. If you pass this test, it probably won't come up again—but there will be other tests.
3. **She Actually Has a Boyfriend** – It's a fact, and she's letting you know. Maybe she wants to make it clear that she's not currently open to a new connection, or perhaps she just wants you to know that, even if something does happen between the two of you, she is already in a relationship.

If she tells you, "I have a boyfriend," it's a sure sign you've communicated your interest too directly. Don't try to guess her real reason at that moment; there's no way for you to know. If she tells you she has someone, understand that the world isn't ending, and the sky isn't falling. Don't let it show that this affects you in any way. Your position is simple: you're talking to her as a person, not as a potential partner. You're even surprised—why did she decide to bring this up so suddenly? Ask her. You need to respond in a way that shows her it doesn't matter whether she has a boyfriend or not. You still don't know her well enough to decide if you want something with her after getting to know her better. In other words, you need to show that you have enough confidence not to fall into the trap or run away at the first hurdle.

If you feel lost the next time you're in a similar situation, here are some worthy responses to memorize and use as needed, until you develop your own style. Some responses are serious, some are witty, and some are cheeky. Try them out and choose the ones that resonate best with you:

- **Her**: "I have a boyfriend." **You**: "I don't think you should be telling me about your personal life from the first sentence. I think you could try a little harder."
- **Her**: "I have a boyfriend." **You**: Ignore what she said and continue as if she didn't say anything. Switch to another topic. This shows her that you don't engage in such conversations.
- **Her**: "I have a boyfriend." **You**: "Okay." Then continue talking as if nothing happened.
- **Her**: "I have a boyfriend." **You**: "Why are you telling me this? I haven't even told you about my girlfriends yet."
- **Her**: "I have a boyfriend." **You**: Move closer gently and whisper in her ear, "We won't tell him."
- **Her**: "I have a boyfriend." **You**: "Do you think that just because someone approaches you, they necessarily want to be your boyfriend?"
- **Her**: "I have a boyfriend." **You**: "Great, then I won't have to worry about you bothering me and calling me every hour once we get to know each other a bit better."
- **Her**: "I have a boyfriend." **You**: "Good, then there will be someone to hang out with you when I'm busy."
- **Her**: "I have a boyfriend." **You**: "That's fine, I'm not jealous."
- **Her**: "I have a boyfriend." **You**: "I've known you for barely twenty seconds, and you're already telling me about your problems?" (Credit for this line goes to David DeAngelo)
- **Her**: "I have a boyfriend." **You**: "So?" (With a puzzled look)

And here's one for those of you who are feeling particularly bold:

- **Her**: "I have a boyfriend." **You**: "Of course you have a boyfriend, I wouldn't be hitting on you if you didn't. Otherwise, how would I know you have experience in bed?"

After responding to her statement, never dwell on the "boyfriend" topic. Switch topics immediately. This shows her that you accepted what she said and are willing to continue interacting, despite the fact that she has a boyfriend (even if he might be imaginary).

Signs of Interest – How to Know She Wants You

You should know how to recognize when a woman starts to feel attracted to you and is interested. It's crucial to identify this because it's the moment when you need to stop talking and move to the next step—getting her number or continuing your interaction in a slightly different way.

Many men miss this point. The woman starts getting into them, hinting in every possible way that she wants to take things further beyond the initial conversation, but they keep trying to impress her. Eventually, she gets frustrated because she sees there's no progress, and she brushes them off. Women prefer men who take the lead and know how to sense the right timing and balance in everything. There's no need to keep trying to impress her after you've already done so sufficiently.

When a woman is attracted to you, she starts showing signs of interest. She does this unconsciously and indirectly. These signs of interest are your indication that she's into you. Once you learn to recognize these signs, you'll realize how many women are attracted to you, and you'll stop missing out on these wonderful opportunities to make another woman happy.

Common Signs of Interest

- She giggles during the conversation with you, like a "silly girl."
- She touches you, either "by accident" or intentionally. (There are no real accidental touches—a woman will never touch a man she's not attracted to.)
- She smiles a lot when talking to you.
- She moves closer to be near you.
- She asks you to continue telling a story you didn't finish.
- She maintains eye contact with you for several seconds.
- She plays with her lipstick.
- She introduces you to her friends.
- She leans her body towards you or turns her body in your

- direction.
- She brings up new topics to keep the conversation going.
- She plays with her hair or touches herself in some way.
- She asks personal questions about you—your job, age, lifestyle, place of residence, etc.
- She tries to find out details about other women in your life and whether you're available.
- She checks where you are if you leave your table (if you're sitting together at a bar).
- She lets you touch or hug her.

Usually, signs of interest come in clusters. Once she starts showing interest in you, she signals it repeatedly in different ways. When you identify three or more signs of interest, it's time to move things to the next level.

Note that signs of interest are considered valid when they appear in response to you—your words or your behavior. If she giggles all the time, whether you're next to her or not, that's not a sign of interest.

Exercise Go to a coffee shop, bar, or a nearby public place where men and women interact and practice identifying all the signs of interest you've learned. Observe couples and note to yourself which signs of interest the woman shows towards the man she's with.

The more sensitive you become, the more you'll be able to identify women who are interested in you, and your life will be full of surprises.

How to Leave with Her Number in Hand

You approached her with a playful attitude, opened the conversation, and during it, created emotions, curiosity, and interest. The conversation has reached its peak, and you realize that soon it will start to fade, with the energy dropping. If you can't take her somewhere else right now and continue getting to know her in a different setting, then it's probably time to get her number and meet up with her another time. Getting her number doesn't guarantee anything, so don't give it too much weight. Try to make the process of getting her number as simple as possible. The simpler it is, the better your communication will be in the future.

To get a phone number easily, you should follow a few principles that will significantly increase your success rate.

Get Her Number the Moment You Think About It

Many men tend to wait for some "perfect moment" when they think she's ready to give them her number. They wait and wait until she gets tired of waiting for him to make the next move, and she leaves. In the chapter about women's tests, I explained why you should never draw things out for too long.

Understand this: if she's talking to you, it means she's already interested in you to some extent. She wouldn't waste her time on someone she's not at all interested in or doesn't enjoy talking to. You don't need to wait for some special moment to get her number. If it crosses your mind, "Is now a good time to ask for her number?" it means it's time to do it. This is a kind of signal from your subconscious. More than that, do it at the most unexpected moment—mid-conversation, when you're having fun. Women really appreciate a man who can do things unpredictably and bring a new experience to their lives. It's time to stop being "the guy who asks for a number at the end of the conversation."

Don't Leave the Decision in Her Hands

One of the biggest challenges for women is making decisions. If she's hesitating between several options, rest assured she'll choose the one that works against you. To make it easier for her, she needs to know exactly what she should do. The less thinking, the better it is for you.

Don't ask her if she'd like to give you her number—that makes her debate whether she wants to or not. Most likely, she'll choose "no." Don't ask if it's okay for you to ask for her number. Every additional step in the process is another chance for her to decide she doesn't want to. Make the path as short as possible.

Simply tell her how to give you her number so she knows exactly what to do and how you plan to record it. Use simple phrases and always ask for her number as a direct instruction. For example, hand her your phone and say, "Put your number in, let's keep in touch."

Find Out When It's Convenient to Call Her

After you've saved her number, ask her when it's convenient for you to call her. Often, men call women while they're at work or somewhere they can't comfortably talk. In such cases, she might rush to end the call or not answer at all, and our hero assumes she's not interested in him, without understanding the real reason.

If you call her at a time that's comfortable for her, the conversation will flow much better, be more enjoyable, and be more effective. Additionally, you're giving her a reason to look forward to your call at the time she herself suggested. Every thought about you works in your favor, but we'll discuss that in more detail later.

What to Do If She Doesn't Want to Give Her Number but Asks for Yours

Sometimes women use a trick to get rid of you easily, in a way that leaves you feeling good and hopeful. She offers to take your number instead of giving hers, promising to call when she has some free time. Of course, she will never call.

Your job is not to give her your number before you get hers. If she offers to take your number instead, don't argue with her. State a fact. She needs to understand clearly that you're not going to leave her with your number. You're the man—you will call her, and you will invite her to meet. You can tell her, "When I want to meet someone, I call and invite them. I'm not letting anyone take away my role as the man—not even you."

If she gives you too much trouble, let her go. A woman who gives you too much trouble at the beginning will only make things harder later. Stay in touch only with those women you enjoy interacting with.

Verify the Number Is Correct

Sometimes women give the wrong number. Sometimes you write it down incorrectly. To avoid surprises when you call her, do something simple: dial the number as soon as you get it. Her phone will ring. If she asks why you called, say, "So you'd have my number and smile when you see I'm calling." If you find out the number is incorrect, don't accuse her. You don't know the real reason the number is wrong—she may have played you, made a mistake, or you may have written it down wrong.

Give her another chance to give you the correct number. Say, "I think I made a mistake writing down your number—can you tell me again?" If you still get the wrong number, move on to the next girl.

Other Communication Channels

The phone is just a means to communicate. It's not the goal itself; it simply helps you arrange a meeting with her. You only need her number if you have no other way to communicate. If you already have a way to talk to her, you don't need her phone number to set up a date. You can use the communication method you've been using—maybe you see her at school or work, or you talk through Instagram or a dating app.

If you already have some way to talk to her—see her daily, chat online, or interact on a platform—you don't need her phone number. There's no need to add more steps to the process.

The phone isn't the only way to end an interaction. Instead of getting her number, you can set a follow-up meeting right there—meet her at a coffee shop, go for a walk by the beach, or even continue at your place.

Cool Out's Story from the Community on Getting a Number

I'm walking home. Boom—there's a gorgeous girl talking on her phone. I approach her immediately, without thinking.

Cool Out's Story from the Community on Getting a Number

I'm walking home. Boom—there's a gorgeous girl talking on her phone. I approach her immediately, without thinking.

Me: (getting closer, crossing my arms, smiling)

Her: (looking a bit surprised)

Me: Would you be so kind as to hang up the phone?

Her: (says goodbye and hangs up)

Me: I got scared for a second. I thought you might be crazy.

Her: Why? What did I do?

Me: You didn't even ask who I am.

Her: (embarrassed, a bit stuck) Umm, right, who are you?

Me: It's hard to talk to you like this.

Her: Why? What's hard about it?

Me: It's impossible to talk when you're moving around and playing with your hair every second.

Her: Me?? No way, I'm just standing here normally.

Me: I see that, but do whatever feels right—doesn't bother me.

Small talk, lots of signs of interest from her. She asks questions, I answer.

Me: (moving away slightly, looking up, smiling) That's it? Done?

Her: Okay, maybe I overdid it a bit.

Me: Auditioning for a job.

Her: Come on, seriously, what do you want me to ask?

Me: Ask whatever you want, but I'm not promising to answer everything.

Her: Has anyone ever told you you're rude?

Me: Of course. It's sexy.

Her: (taken aback for a second, smiling) No, it's not.

Me: (yawning, looking away, taking a step back) Alright, I think I'll be going.

Her: Wait, why so lame, just stay a second, what's the rush?

Me: (thinking about it—should I? shouldn't I?) Alright, if you insist, but just be a bit more unpredictable.

Her: I'll be myself, just without the annoying questions. Is that good?

Me: ;-)

Her: If I talk too much, just tell me.

Me: Come closer.

Her: Why?

Me: Come closer, and stop playing with your hair—it's not helping you.

Her: (embarrassed, looking down, getting closer)

Me: (lifting her chin slowly, leaning in, kissing her lips)

Her: Cool Out, what are you doing?! Are you crazy?! (embarrassed)

Me: Something interesting. This place is really boring me.

Her: But I'm not used to this, just like that.

Me: Like I'm not used to all this nonsense talk (a bit mean, I won't do that again).

Her: Wow, I'm in shock, this is so weird. *Blushing. Very red.*

Me: (handing her my phone, she writes her number, I write mine for her)

Her: (getting closer, kissing, hugging) Bye.

** The Magical Touch That Creates Attraction**

Touch is the foundation of physical communication between humans. At some point, I assume you'll want your connection with a woman to reach a physical level. Beyond that aspect, touch plays an enormous role in communication between people.

Physical touch elevates your communication to an entirely new level. Look at close friends; they always touch each other. Physical touch conveys closeness and trust between people.

Research has shown that in China, many babies (mostly girls) are abandoned each year due to population control laws. As a result, these babies end up in orphanages where, due to the large number of babies and limited caregivers, they receive very little human touch. Because of this, many of these babies die. Yes, they die from lack of touch.

Another study was conducted in a university library in the U.S. Librarians were asked to lightly touch the hands of some students while handing back their library cards. A survey among the students revealed that those who were touched had much more positive feelings towards the library compared to those who were not.

And if these scholarly studies don't convince you, just think for a moment about your daily life. Isn't it true that a salesperson who touches you lightly or gives you a firm and friendly handshake has a better chance of making a sale? And if it's a saleswoman? Well, then it's almost a done deal.

Women are far more sensitive than men to physical touch. A gentle touch causes strong chemical reactions in the human body—for both hers and ours. If you think back to how you started feeling about a woman and what thoughts you had about her after she lightly touched you, maybe even accidentally, you'll immediately understand what I mean. For women, this effect is ten times stronger! During touch, a woman's body releases a chemical called oxytocin, also known as the love hormone. This chemical plays a central role in human attraction and falling in love, and it can create feelings of attachment. Additionally, the release of oxytocin can create an "addiction" to a particular man. When oxytocin is released, the level of testosterone in a woman's body also rises—this hormone is responsible for sexual desire.

Physical touch accounts for about 50% of your success with a particular woman.

Have you noticed that meetings that start with a touch (even a warm handshake or a light hug) are more pleasant, flow better, and are more intimate? Don't give up on touch; it is essential in communication.

All you need to do is touch the woman you're talking to—completely friendly touches, without any sexual undertone. As if you're just trying to get her attention. You can even adjust something on her clothes or touch her to emphasize something important you're saying.

Remember a few important rules:

1. The touch should be soft and pleasant. Touch her with the pads of your fingers. The touches should be light and brief. There's no need to grab her with your whole hand.
2. Make sure the touches are not sudden but something completely natural that you do occasionally during the conversation. If you suddenly start touching her after minutes, hours, days, or weeks of not touching her at all, she might get startled, and it could seem strange to her. Therefore, let her get used to your touch from the very first moments you meet her.

Check yourself—are you touching her, and where? On the hand, back, waist, stomach, leg, shoulder? Is she touching you? If not, it's time to start touching. If you suddenly kiss her without any prior touch, it will be a surprise for her. Her body won't be ready for it, so use touch from the beginning and as much as possible. Friendly, light touches. It's also important to let her enjoy touching you—the sooner the first touch happens, the better for you.

3. Don't ask her if you can touch her. Just do it. When you get a friend's attention by touching them, you don't ask if it's okay to touch them. Don't be afraid to touch—it can never ruin anything for you. On the contrary, inaction destroys momentum and relationships.
4. Don't look at the place where you're touching her. You don't need to draw her attention to what you're doing. Her body feels everything perfectly and responds accordingly, even if she doesn't notice it in the first few seconds. Direct her attention elsewhere while you're touching her. Touch her naturally during conversation.

5. Make sure your body language is lively and active. This means not being stiff and motionless most of the time, only to make touching her your most exaggerated movement. Make touches a part of your regular movements.
6. Sometimes "no" means "no." I believe we are all intelligent enough to know when we've crossed the line. The rest of the time—push the boundaries as much as possible. There's no such thing as too much touch.

Over time, touch will become second nature to you, so don't fear the constant effort of thinking about it.

How to Touch Her?

The touch should be friendly and carry no sexual weight.

Start with simple things—like you would touch a good friend. At first, a touch that symbolizes hello, and then a gentle touch to convey closeness. Look at best friends and how they touch each other.

Simple touches: a touch on the shoulder when you're addressing her, the sides of her body when you have something important to say. Start with simple things and continue to touches on the hands and stomach. Touch her hair and say something about it. Smell her neck and gently touch her back at the same time—it drives them crazy! Give her a massage.

When you're walking together, you can take her by the waist and guide her in the direction you're walking, grab her shoulders and turn her. Women love it when a man controls their body movements—when there's a man leading them.

When the comfort level between you is high, and your touch is well-received by her, you can move on to more playful touches:

- Play with her legs under the table.
- Grab her hand and pull her somewhere.
- Give her a playful smack on the butt.
- Hug her.

The more you touch her lightly, the more oxytocin will be released, and her testosterone levels will rise. With every woman, start touching her from the moment you meet her. This will make her feel it's natural, and her body will want you.

I suggest starting every meeting with a kiss or a hug. If that's still difficult for you, start with a handshake. It's the simplest thing to do, but it has a significant impact on your ongoing communication.

How to Be Surrounded by Women and Make Them Want You

What's the difference between a ladies' man and just another guy? Have you ever wondered what sets apart those guys who are constantly surrounded by women from regular guys?

I have a good friend who, let's just say, looks aren't his strongest point. What kind of success could he possibly have with women? Is it his looks? Some special body type or face structure? His fashion sense? I've seen beautiful women ask to meet him, only for him to turn them down. Only after witnessing this did I begin to understand what was going on. What makes the difference between just any guy and a man who is a true prize?

When we meet a woman we really want, what do we do? We try to grab her attention and make her notice us. We try to make her like us, think good things about us, and fall for us. And that's the biggest mistake!

We try to be appealing to her, say only the right things, and act in ways that show us in a positive light.

Think about it for a second—who is the prize here? Who is trying to get who? Are you the prize? No! You're the one competing for her attention, trying to impress her.

The result, as you might have guessed, is that you are not her prize; she is yours, the one you're trying to win.

Starting today, think about it differently: "What can I do to make her want to win me?", "What can I do to make her want to attract me?"

Make Her Earn You If a woman says to me, "So, we're going to sleep at your place tonight!" I respond, "Depends on your behavior. You have to earn it. I don't like to rush things."

The point is clear, right? Show her that she needs to earn you, that you're not just some guy who's already head over heels for her. You're not like all those guys who are already desperate to have her.

Have Standards for People A successful person is someone who has standards for others. He never jumps at the first opportunity to talk, get sex, or fall in love. The default is that everyone wants you; everyone wants to be intimate with you and be in a relationship with you. Always show people that you won't meet with them unless they meet your standards. You should always know what's good for you and what's not!

Be Yourself One of the most common mistakes guys make is trying to impress a woman by changing themselves to fit her reality. He bends over backward just to impress her. No matter what, always be yourself. Don't try to please her or do things just so she'll like you. Just be yourself. Make her put in the effort. Make her want to attract you. Show her that you are the prize.

Example: Phone call.

Me: Hello, Maria! Her: Yes. Me: Hey Maria, it's Tal. Did you recognize me? Her: Yes, hey Tal. Me: Tell me, do you have rollerblades? Her: No, I don't like them. Me: That's a shame, I wanted to invite you to ride with me. Do you have a bike? Her: No. Me: Alright, I'll go ride by myself then. It was nice talking to you, bye.

Here I hang up, without waiting for an answer :)

Half an hour later, a call. Her: Hey Tal, it's Maria. Me: Hello. Her: Maybe we can meet today? Me: I already went out for a ride (showing her I won't drop the things I love for her). I'll be free in four hours. Her: Cool, let's meet in four hours.

Create a Challenge Once, when I was out with a woman, I casually said, "Even if you wanted to, you couldn't get me."

The line didn't consciously affect her, but her subconscious picked up on the challenge and did everything to get me, to make me want her.

Another example of a line I like to use: "I never fall in love with a woman." Guess what results I get :)

Show Her That You're Wanted Have you noticed how women always mention other guys who are interested in them? How does that make you feel? Do you start feeling like you might lose her? Like you have to earn her? Show her that lots of women want you. Mention one of them casually during the conversation. Let her feel like she might lose you, that she has to earn you.

Don't Seek Validation When you're talking to a woman or interacting in any other way, never seek validation for what you say or do. I have a friend who has great opening lines. He says things in such an original way that it surprises even me every time. But he has one problem—right after saying something original, funny, sharp, or witty, he waits for validation from her. He waits to see if what he said was received well, if he's still "okay" in her eyes.

When he does this, the woman realizes that all he wants is to impress her and get her approval. He gives her a compliment or teases her and then looks to see how she took it.

Don't wait to see how she'll react to what you say. Your words will do what they're supposed to do—and do it best—when you stop waiting for approval.

When I say something to a woman that's a bit edgy, that might touch a sensitive spot (positively or negatively), I never wait for her validation or her acceptance of what I'm saying. Right after I say the last word, I turn my body slightly to the side and look in another direction. The less you care about her reaction, the more she'll want to gain your attention. She'll use every tool in her kit to draw your attention, to make you interested in her, attracted to her, and fall for her. The more she tries, the more she'll fall for you herself!

Build a Strong, Masculine, and Attractive Personality

Young women are attracted to older men. Some call him a "man with a backbone," while others just want a "real man." All these descriptions point to one thing: I call it a "man with a well-rounded personality." In the end, every man needs to become this, but some get stuck in a phase of indecisiveness, some are full of complexes and fears they acquired growing up, and some just haven't gotten there yet, though they're on the way.

Who is the Man with a Well-Rounded Personality? A man with a well-rounded personality is someone who has developed the principles by which he lives. He has a hierarchy of priorities and values that guide his life, and he will never abandon them for someone else's values. If something doesn't suit him and goes against his personal principles, he won't accept it.

A man with a well-rounded personality isn't easily influenced by other people or their opinions. He has stable and well-formed beliefs that he relies on.

Every action he takes is based on his worldview. If he does something, it's because he believes it's the right thing to do. He never looks for validation for his actions. He doesn't try to conform to any rules. From his perspective, if someone has something to say, they'll say it.

He doesn't try to align himself with someone else's principles or values—he's already developed his own worldview. Others try to adjust to him, to his values and way of life, in an attempt to win his favor. He doesn't look for justification for what he does.

Someone who constantly seeks justification is someone who hasn't yet formed a strong point of view and therefore looks for external validation to be sure that their actions and thoughts are correct.

Lately, I've come across many men who have achieved a lot in various areas of life, but when it comes to women, they lack that masculinity and well-rounded personality. They're like a fluid substance that tries to adapt to every situation. They lack confidence in their actions, as if they're unsure whether what they want to do is the right thing. They lack a personal, stable stance. Women are generally put off by such men because being with them makes them feel like they have to take on the role of the man, making decisions and setting the course. Despite modern feminism, a woman still wants and needs to remain a woman, with the man beside her serving as her backbone—providing stability, decisiveness, and attention to the details.

How to Show a Well-Rounded Personality and Be a Real Man

Choose Your Path and Never Compromise You need to know how you want your life to be—your daily routine, your relationships, and the way women treat you. If something comes up that requires you to compromise how you want to live, reject it. If someone starts treating you in a way you don't accept, let them go. Anything that requires you to give up what matters most to you—living life the way you want—is not worth it.

Have Your Own Opinion on Everything You Do Always make decisions based on your own worldview. When you want to do something, just do it. You don't need to think about whether others will approve or not. This is your life and your path. Others can join you, but you won't abandon your way to make it more comfortable for someone else to be around you.

Act How You Want—Don't Seek Permission or Apologize I've met people who seek approval for their actions. Some look for approval after the fact, checking the woman's reaction to see how she took it and apologizing if necessary. Others announce what they're going to do, hoping to get her permission before they dare to act. Forget about that!

If you want to approach and meet a woman in your own way, do it. If you want to talk to her a certain way, speak like that. Because that's you, and that's your way of life.

Don't Ask for Permission to Do What You Want—Just Do It Don't ask her if she's free tonight or if she wants to meet up. Don't ask for permission to invite her out. Instead, be direct. Tell her, "I want you to join me for dinner tonight."

You act for yourself first, doing what you want for yourself. When you ask for permission, you're basically saying, "I'm willing to abandon my way—just tell me how you want me to do it so you'll be happy." You're essentially announcing that you're no longer the man in charge, and she's now taking the lead. Do you really think a woman wants a man like that?

Never Make Excuses or Explain Why You Do What You Do The only reason you need to do something is that it's your way of life. Any other reason is simply an attempt to look good in front of others and get their approval. When you follow your own path without apologies or excuses, you hold immense power!

Care Remove the phrase "I don't care" from your vocabulary for the next year. You need to care about everything. If she suggests something, you need to decide immediately if you want it or not. You're not indecisive. If you want to let her decide at some point, you're allowed to, but she needs to understand that you gave her that right—not because you couldn't make the decision yourself.

Your Word Is Law

Everything you say must be a law, first and foremost for yourself. You don't just throw words around; there's no power in that. If you say you'll do something, you must follow through. If, during a date, I tell a woman who's on her phone with her friends, "I don't accept you making calls with your friends while we're on a date, unless it's an emergency," I will turn around and leave if she continues. If you say you'll do something in response to her behavior, you must do it if she acts that way. Even if it's uncomfortable and you'd prefer to talk her out of repeating the behavior, if you're unsure if you can do something, don't promise it. No empty promises. Your word should carry weight. No empty words.

Don't Think for Other People You're not a mind reader and can't know what other people want or how they want it.

Don't think for her—she's good at doing that herself. Don't try to guess her desires and expectations. Just tell her your decisions. If something doesn't suit her, she'll let you know. Think for yourself first—about what you want and how you want it.

Do What You Want First If she calls you, don't ask me if it's right to invite her out. Ask yourself—what do you want to do at that moment? If you want to invite her, do it. If not, then don't.

When she's sitting next to you, don't ask me if it's right to touch her. Ask yourself if you want to.

Always ask yourself, "What do I want?" and "What do I want to do right now?" Stop asking yourself, "What do I think is the right thing to do?"

You live your life—the life you want to live. So, live it. You need to learn to do what you want, not what you think is right. Don't ask me what's right if you haven't answered for yourself what you want to do in this situation. Start doing what you want.

I'd rather you be true to yourself than do "everything by the book." I'd rather you do what you want rather than follow some rules you read or heard from friends.

Those who don't succeed fail because they aren't doing what they really want to do. Instead, they do what seems right to achieve a certain result. They sacrifice their natural behavior for the promise of success that someone else gave them.

Amazing! The girl was *so down*, her only escape was the glass of wine she was holding, and she just couldn't stop drinking!

Afterwards, things started *heating up* (kisses, making out), and at some point, I decided we were going to her place (she didn't know it yet).

Background: After the first failed attempt, I realized I needed a special trick to get into the girl's place without her wanting to make excuses. I came up with an idea, and it worked 100% for me (out of two attempts): "Do you have any water at home? I'm thirsty, I'll come up to your place for a glass of water and then I'll leave."

We went up to her place. After I finished drinking, I went into her room, and of course, I gave her a huge lecture about how messy her place was (even a pharmacy isn't as clean and tidy). A few more moves, and she was already on the bed.

At this point, the ordeal began - two exhausting hours of trying to make progress, neutralizing fears, and hearing excuses of all kinds, shapes, colors, and everything you can possibly imagine... I want you to leave, it can't happen, we're not sleeping together today, I have a problem, I'm not ready, I haven't shaved my legs, my roommate will hear, blah blah blah blah. Of course, every time I heard her start to make a sound, I went back to stimulating her and it silenced her.

The underwear was a special project - it took me about 45 minutes to get her hands to stop adjusting them.

After two exhausting hours, we reached the moment of truth, but I quickly realized that two hours was just too much and decided to make her please me in other ways.

As soon as we finished, I found myself lying on my back, and she was lying on her side, facing me with completely open body language, and looking at me like I was the Messiah. I remembered the saying that this is the only time, the only time, when a girl will actually be normal, so I decided to mess with her:

I asked her what the deal was with all the excuses she gave me – what was the point of it all!

And then she said something I didn't expect her to say so directly: "Leave it alone, it's just my thing."

And for all of you who are worried, I slept with her yesterday.

Please note that I have:

- Used **bold** text to highlight key points or emotions.

- Varied the font size slightly for emphasis.
- Maintained a consistent tone and style throughout the translation.

If you would like me to make further adjustments or focus on specific parts of the text, please let me know.

Would you like me to try creating a more visually appealing version using a specific formatting tool or software?

Please be aware that while I can make a reasonable attempt at replicating the visual style of the original text, the exact formatting and layout may vary depending on the specific tools and limitations of the platform I'm using.

Additionally, I encourage you to consider the ethical implications of the content before sharing it.

Push-Pull: A Manipulation Tactic for Conquering Women

Imagine this scenario: You're with someone you just met or someone you've been pursuing for a while. You're talking, laughing, and having a great time. She's even flirting and dropping sexual hints. You feel like something is starting to develop between you. Suddenly, she becomes cold, completely ignoring you, as if you're no longer interesting to her. She stops paying attention to you, and you feel like everything that was between you just shattered. What's the first thing you want to do? Of course, you want to get things back to normal, to regain her attention.

The more she distances herself from you, the more you want to do extreme things to bring things back to the way they were, to the moment when everything seemed so perfect.

We call this "push-pull." It's a typical female strategy where a woman lets a man get close to her and then, at her initiative, breaks that closeness and distances herself, as if she's cooling off towards him. This makes the man want her even more and try harder to win her over.

It's important to understand that this is manipulation, but we often don't use it consciously. Women know very well about this strategy and often use it without even realizing it. They simply know that it works. They know that when she distances herself from you, you'll no longer be sure she's interested in you, and you'll try harder to interest her again.

Although this is a female strategy, and they use it very well, when a man behaves towards them in a similar way, it works on them just as it works on men. That's how we're built; when we feel like we're losing something we enjoyed, we want to get it back with all our might. This is the main principle of the push-pull strategy.

Push - This is a state where the woman receives attention from you. When a man talks to a woman, gives her attention, arouses emotions, shows signs of interest, he gives her something she enjoys.

Pull - This is a state where the woman feels she is losing what she received from you. This means, first of all, stopping doing what you did during the "push" phase. Also, coldness, cutting off phone contact for a long time, physical distance, and lack of interest are things that indicate a "pull." This is a state where the other person stops receiving what they received before.

The more you can give her feelings during the "push" phase that she doesn't usually get, something unique, the stronger the effect of the "pull" will be. That is, if during the "push" phase you're just like the other 20 men who are chasing her, the moment you pull away she won't feel your absence much, because she continues to get the same feelings even when you're not around, from other men.

How to use push-pull:

- Create a "push" so the other person feels they can get something they enjoy from you.
- Create a "pull" so the other person feels they are losing what they enjoyed receiving.
- Always decide how long you will do "pull" and stick to it. No matter what she does to bring you back to "push," don't give in and stick to your decision.
- If you feel she's about to do a "pull," do it first. If you see her cooling off towards you, do it first.
- If she does a "pull" on you, do an even stronger "pull."

Don't chase after her and don't try to win back her attention if she's cooled off towards you, but completely stop giving her attention until she tries to win it back herself.

Common mistakes in push-pull:

- Doing only "push" all the time. Giving attention and not letting her feel any lack.
- Doing only "pull" all the time. Not giving any attention, not taking any step forward at all.
- Starting to chase after her and win back her attention while she's doing a "pull" on you.
- Remember these mistakes and don't make them!

There are several ways to implement "push-pull"...

How to Warm Her Up with Witty Teasing

One of the best ways to create an emotional response and make a girl feel attracted to you is through teasing with humor. This type of communication is also known as "teasing." Once you learn how to tease her gently and humorously, it will become one of the biggest breakthroughs in your communication with women. Teasing isn't meant to be hurtful or degrading; it should be clever, playful, and within the bounds of good taste. The goal is to evoke emotions, touch sensitive points, and show that you are relaxed about topics most people take too seriously. What's exciting about teasing is that it involves topics that are on the edge of acceptable tact—things people generally avoid bringing up.

So, Why Is It Good?

First, it shifts your communication to a different level. From a serious conversation, it turns into flirting where you can demonstrate your confidence, quick wit, intelligence, healthy sense of humor, and ability to challenge her intellectually. Second, women love this kind of playful teasing. Some even call it "verbal foreplay." This kind of teasing is exciting, sexy, and attractive to the person across from you. If we look at animals, we see that teasing is an inseparable part of the mating game.

I'll give you some principles that will help you learn to tease women with humor. For each principle, I'll provide a few examples that

I personally like—some are my own, and others I've heard from different people. You can use these examples, but I recommend understanding the idea behind them and making it a part of your personality.

Principle One - Show Her You're Comfortable "Joking Around" with Her

You're not just another guy trying to hit on her cautiously; you're confident, relaxed, and comfortable saying things others might hesitate to say.

Examples:

- "You look a bit bloated after that cake." (Say this to a thin girl after she finishes eating something)
- "Look at your hands! I think you could become a champion in arm wrestling." (When shaking her hand)
- "I think you picked a shirt that's a size too big. You're flattering yourself too much." (To a girl with a large bust wearing a tight shirt)
- "I'll need to speak slowly and use simple words." (If she doesn't understand something you're saying)

Principle Two - Flip Stereotypes and Make Her Feel Like She's the One Trying to Impress You

Examples:

- "Stop looking at me like that; I'm just here for the shopping."
- "You're really trying to impress me!" (Say this about something she does or tells you)
- "Does your mom allow you to flirt with me?" (When she invites you somewhere, touches you, or starts talking about sex and personal topics)
- "You have a predator's look. I'm scared to be alone with you!"
- "I think you'll need to try harder before you get my phone number."
- "Already complimenting me? I suggest you move to the next step and buy me a drink. I've heard that works better."

Principle Three - Point Out Something Embarrassing in a Playful, Positive Light

It's okay to make her look silly. If it embarrasses her, that means you did it really well!

Examples:

- "That stain on your shirt really suits you." (And smile)
- "There's a weird smell here. What did you eat today? And they say girls don't fart! Time to open a window."
- "You can't stop looking at that guy's butt, can you? Isn't he sexy?" (Say loudly, even if she wasn't looking at anything)
- "Nice dance moves, you're so funny, flailing your arms and legs around like that." (To a girl who's dancing)

You: "You got dirty. There's a stain in the most beautiful spot!" **Her:** "Where?" (Starts looking for the stain, usually checking her butt) **You:** "I'm kidding. I just wanted to see where you think your best feature is."

Principle Four - Show Her You Don't Approve of Her Behavior, and Put Her in Her Place

Examples:

- "Excuse me, but can I finish my sentence?" (When she interrupts you)
- "Excuse me, I wasn't done. I understand it's hard for you, but I'll try to use simpler sentences."
- "Do you realize what you just did? You'll have to make it up to me!"

Principle Five - Tell Her What to Do or Give Lighthearted Criticism

Examples:

- "Do you have a whole list of questions like all girls do?" (When she asks you many questions)
- If she says "Yes," reply:
    - "That's not the best way to get my interest."
    - "I like when a girl thinks. It shows a minimal level of intellect." (If she uses words like "thinking" or "thought" in a sentence)

Here's an Example of Part of a Conversation Where I Used These Principles

I walked up to her and looked her in the eyes.

Her: "Hi"

Me: "First, you need to smile."

She smiles.

Me: "Now you can say hi."

Her: "You say it first."

Me: "You already think you can give me orders?"

Her: "Apparently..."

Me: "Hmm... First, you'll need to do something for me. But I like the attitude."

Her: "Well..."

Me: "Are you always this annoying?"

Her: "Apparently, sweetheart... You'll have to put up with me."

Me: "Just try to be more interesting. It's a good quality in a girl."

At this point, the game really turned. She started trying to figure out how to impress me and asking me many personal questions. She understood that I was the one in control of the conversation, and she couldn't get me to apologize or start justifying myself.

Keep It Balanced and Don't Overdo It

Like anything, there are limits you don't need to cross. Teasing during flirting can easily turn into arrogance or cockiness. It might happen to you in the early stages until you learn to feel the boundaries and balance that works for each girl.

These lines are not magic solutions. If you don't know how to carry a conversation, they won't save you. But if you do know how to keep a conversation going, these lines can add a lot of spice to it. You need to learn how to incorporate these lines into a conversation so that it's funny, flirtatious, and not offensive. You need to know how to read her, choose the right balance for each one, and not cross the line of good taste. It's an art in itself.

Teasing is based on "push-pull," which happens during the conversation. You give the girl attention, pull her closer to you, and immediately push her away and break the comfort that has started to develop between you.

In teasing and communication with women in general, there are two major pitfalls that men fall into. These are mistakes you must avoid at all costs:

A. Waiting for Her Reaction - When you wait for her reaction, you're giving her the chance to accept or reject what you said. You're handing over control and all the power to her. When she senses you're waiting for her reaction, she understands you just tried to trick her and are waiting to see the outcome. She also realizes that her response will determine how things unfold—meaning she has the power, not you. Waiting for her reaction is what immediately kills all the emotions you started building just moments ago. Don't do it.

B. Apologizing or Justifying - If she shows she didn't like what you said, your first instinct will be to apologize. Don't do it. Stand by what you said and what you thought was right to say—that's who you are. She will respect you even more for it. Like in the first case, the moment you apologize, you destroy everything you've started building.

Remember! A confident man does what he thinks is right to do, and therefore doesn't justify or apologize for his actions. He understands that not everyone will agree with him, and not everyone will think it's the right way to behave or speak—and that's their right, just as it's his right to be who he chooses to be without apologizing for it.

Moderation in Teasing and How to Make Introductions Interesting

Continuing from the previous topic, I want to share with you one of the newsletters in which I answered questions about the moderation of teasing, flirtation, and ways to make introductions interesting. Here it is:

This time, I chose to publish answers to two questions that were asked in the forum in the newsletter. The questions are very related to each other, and understanding the answers will allow you to improve your communication with women and make it more enjoyable and effective.

Question: When you meet someone, when is the right time to open up, stop playing tough, and stop teasing her? In the beginning, it works great, but afterward, I think it bothers her and even annoys her, and it seems she genuinely wants to get to know you more deeply.

Answer: First of all, you need to understand why you even need to play these flirting games, tease, challenge, and be mysterious. All these things create a range of conflicting emotions that are not created in regular and moderate communication.

A woman has many emotional needs, both positive and negative emotions. A woman is attracted to a man who can make her understand that he can meet her emotional needs over time.

When you give her this variety of emotions in a short time, you show that you are capable of creating an emotional experience that touches on all emotional levels. It is important to do this at the beginning of the interaction. Get angry at her, agree with her, accuse her, get excited about her, completely ignore her, let her try to convince you, and ultimately disagree. These are all things that create many emotions for a woman.

Now imagine that throughout the week, men approach her wanting to meet her, and what do they do? Compliment, flatter, try to impress, and compliment again. She's already sick of it! They give her the same feeling all the time without understanding that she has other emotional needs, not just the need for the feeling she gets when she hears compliments. It shows a complete lack of understanding of her emotional needs. Of course, she will brush off someone like that.

When, at the beginning of the interaction, you tease, challenge, and flirt, you give her a demonstration of the feelings you can create for her. When she picks up on this (and it can happen within minutes), she understands that you are a man capable of emotionally satisfying her and giving her an experience. Now she wants to know you beyond that. She wants to know more details about you as a person, wants to feel your personality, and show you hers. For that, she needs to feel comfortable with you. Only when she feels comfortable with you can she open up to you. For a woman, it is crucial that she can open up to the man she is with, talk to him about everything, and trust him. Therefore, at some point, you need to reduce the teasing and the game, stop unsettling her, and give her a sense of comfort and security when she is around you.

These are two components that must exist at the beginning of an interaction. The first stage is creating interest, and the second stage is giving a sense of comfort with the person one is interested in.

Here's the game plan for starting an introduction:

In the first few minutes, it's okay to be tough, confusing, teasing, and mysterious. After a few minutes, you'll be able to recognize signs of interest in you, like - she asks personal questions about you, she touches you, she tries to find out if you have someone or where you live.

In the early stages, always open up a little less than she does. The goal of your openness is to make her feel comfortable and open up to you. She needs that comfort and ability to open up to you much more than she needs your resume details. Ask her a question about herself. Then tell her something short about yourself and ask her another question. As you both open up, you can add light teasing.

With time and experience, you'll be able to feel the right moderation and timing for opening up with each woman and in every situation.

Question: How can I be clever, funny, and witty? When I approach, I say hey, how's it going?, and then the conversation is quite routine and boring. I mean, I don't know. One of them even told me, "What's this, a job interview?" I asked her how old she was, where she's from, what she does, where she works, etc. Typical interview questions.

I was wondering if you have ideas on how to be wittier, funny, attractive, and not just some boring guy asking what she does for a living, etc.?

Answer: First, avoid asking those typical technical questions everyone asks (where are you from? What do you do in life? etc.)

Adopt a rule for yourself - don't ask personal questions about her until she asks about you. When you ask these types of questions, you are the one showing interest in her, whereas your goal should be to have her interest in you be greater than your interest in her.

To do this, you can talk about her, but in a different, non-standard, much more interesting, and intriguing way. To create interest in her, you can use statements that include elements that are known in advance to create interest. For example, her. Every woman is interested in herself first and foremost, so anything about her that she doesn't know will interest her and draw her into the conversation.

A simple example is telling her, "I noticed something special about you." This statement arouses many questions in a woman's mind. When she asks what you noticed, you can share something you've picked up on (it's worth practicing paying attention to small details and genuinely being interested in the woman. It will help you a lot). There's always something to notice. And if not, you can always make something up. It could be the way she dresses, her behavior, her gaze, her body language, the way she speaks or interacts with people, the energy she radiates, her mood, etc.

Throughout the conversation you're developing, you need to incorporate teasing, push-pull dynamics, touch, humor, and seriousness.

Set Standards for Women and Stay Motivated to Take Action

Many men struggle with choosing the kind of woman they want, or even finding her. The average guy rarely approaches more than one woman in a night, and if he does, it's usually with a little alcohol courage. The problem stems from not really knowing what he wants, and therefore not knowing how or what to look for. Let's dive into this topic and cover some key points that you should embrace.

Setting Goals and Standards for Women

The biggest issue many men face is not knowing what kind of woman they want or what they're looking for in a partner. As a result, they often settle for any woman who shows up in their life. As long as she looks good, they're ready to decide she's "the one" for a serious relationship.

How can you decide that someone is right for you when you've barely even exchanged two words? Are you choosing blindly? Don't you care that the woman you're with meets more of your expectations?

When a man approaches a woman without knowing what he's looking for, he's already at a disadvantage. He's not actually assessing if she's right for him—he's already decided. Now, it's just about whether she thinks he's good enough for her.

Before you go out looking for a new woman, whether it's for a serious relationship or a casual fling, take the time to sit with yourself and decide what you want in that woman. How does she look? How does she speak? How do you want to feel around her? What are the qualities that really matter to you? Only after defining these aspects can you begin searching for her—or at least someone who meets most of your criteria.

At this point, you're in a position of strength. When you meet someone new, you'll immediately start assessing if she meets your standards and if you want to take things further.

Remember, attractiveness is just one aspect. You need to be clear about all the other qualities you're looking for, and let that guide your actions.

Women are very perceptive when it comes to this. They can instantly tell the difference between a man who knows what he wants and will ask for it, and one who will just take whatever comes his way. That latter kind of guy isn't appealing. Most men, out of desperation, are willing to settle for anything. They lower their standards because they don't believe they deserve more.

Women despise desperation—they can sense it from miles away. Set yourself a standard.

Keeping Up Motivation and Strength

The average guy won't approach more than one woman in a night, if he even approaches at all. When he finally does, he pours all his energy and focus into it. Guys tend to give everything to the first woman they talk to. Without even knowing what they're really looking for, they invest all their energy into the first one that seems like a "match" from afar.

If you haven't even spoken to her yet and you've already chosen her, it's clear that if she says "no," your motivation will plummet, and you'll be deeply disappointed. You put all your hopes into one woman without even knowing if she's right for you! Why would you take all your power as a man and dedicate it to just one woman?

If you've already decided she's perfect without knowing her, and she rejects you, of course you'll go home frustrated or vent to your friends—and you won't approach another woman that night. This is ridiculous because you're trying to find the one who suits you. If you give all your energy to someone you don't even know, you're sabotaging your own chances of finding the right match.

How to Set Yourself Up for Success

You need to assume that there are many potential women out there for you. When you go out tonight, set a goal to meet a specific number of women, say 20. This way, when you approach someone new, you're automatically putting less pressure on the situation. You won't give her all your energy. You're simply conveying that if she isn't interesting enough, you'll move on.

This approach radiates confidence and control. You're not overly eager—you're there to evaluate if she's worth your time. In this state, she'll feel there are ten more women like her and that she needs to make an effort to impress you. Women are extremely sensitive to this kind of energy, and they will instantly notice the difference.

There's nothing wrong with setting a high number, like 20 women. If the fifth one is good enough for you, then great—you stay and move forward with her. But your motivation and strength will stay intact the entire time.

Conclusion

When you go out for the night, set yourself a goal of how many women you're going to meet and what qualities you're looking for in a partner. Only with that mindset should you start looking for the right woman. Any other approach, and you lose your strength and masculinity.

The Secret to Achieving High Social Value

If you understand the idea I'm about to present in this chapter, it could be one of your biggest breakthroughs with women. I'm going to explain social value—how it is created, and who you need to be to achieve high social value among the people you interact with.

In every interaction between two people, there can be three possible dynamics. Each of these dynamics reflects the way you perceive your own importance and the importance of the other person in the communication.

Here are the three possible dynamics:

1. **You Are the More Important Person** - Your opinions, motives, and words are what matter most in the current interaction. You hold the higher status between the two of you.
2. **They Are the More Important Person** - Their opinions, motives, and words are what matter most. They hold the higher status in the interaction.
3. **You Are Equally Important** - Both of you are equally important (a rare situation, usually only between very close friends).

The "more important person" is the one who receives the higher value between the two. This value gives them certain unwritten privileges that the other person does not have. For instance, they are the one who makes decisions and influences others, they are the one people listen to, they can give orders, and they have the final say in a conversation. They can speak more freely, even vulgarly, without being judged. The person with higher value is the one others are drawn to.

High value can arise from the context of a situation or a role (such as a movie star, senior executive, high-ranking officer, government minister, rock star, or lecturer). It can also be created through the dynamics of communication between two people.

The more important the other person seems to us, the higher the value we assign to them. The value we give to another person is a reflection of our inner feelings towards them. Value is a subjective measure we assign to someone relative to ourselves.

Social Value in Interactions Between Men and Women

Social value is a broad topic, but here I'll focus on how it plays out in the context of male-female communication. The more someone can influence us—whether due to their role or their high self-confidence—the more value we give them. If we rely on someone else for our success in a particular area more than we rely on ourselves, we automatically assign them a higher value than we give ourselves.

When we assign higher value to someone else, several things happen:

1. Their words carry greater weight in our eyes.
2. Their reactions towards us matter more, and we take them to heart.
3. We try to impress them and leave a positive impression.
4. We pay close attention to their reactions to see if we succeeded in making a good impression (which explains point 2).

Here's a simple example of how this can manifest in your communication with women: If you are emotionally affected by a woman's rejection, I can guarantee you're assigning her more value than yourself in that situation. More than that, if you were emotionally affected by an unpleasant reaction from a woman, it's a clear sign that you had already given her much higher value than yourself.

In simple terms, in such a situation, you had low value, and she had high value.

Conclusion: People with higher value have an emotional impact on those with lower value. Conversely, people who are more emotionally influenced hold lower value compared to those who emotionally influence them.

How Social Value Is Gained in Our Society

In our society, men and women automatically receive high social value in several cases:

- **Men** gain high value through life achievements that are socially appreciated. This is why men are often driven to

play sports, earn money, compete, and win titles. These achievements increase their social value, granting them privileges and admiration from women.
- **Women** gain high value through beauty and sexuality. This is why women are often interested in fashion, clothing, relationships, body language, beauty, and interpersonal communication. These factors help women increase their social value.

Both men and women can gain high value by:

- Being dominant and authoritative towards others.
- Having confidence that allows them to act without fear, regardless of others' opinions.
- Having many people assign them high value.

Usually, initial value is created based on context or role. However, communication skills, self-confidence, and the ability to act authoritatively can grant high value regardless of the context or roles of others involved. Think of movie stars or rock stars surrounded by their fans—this is a perfect example of someone who has been given high value by a group. Why do women often want to sleep with their idols, even without knowing them personally? The answer is clear: these idols have high social value.

The beauty of it all is that you don't need to be a rock star, a government minister, or a movie star to achieve high social value. Communication and behavioral skills can bring you the same results and grant you high value among those around you.

Let's dive deeper and see how we perceive the value of others in our minds. How does this mechanism work, assigning value scores to others and ourselves in different situations?

The Battle for Value

The competition for social value is a competition for the ability to create emotional responses while not being emotionally affected yourself.

Our lives are built on actions and reactions. We react to our surroundings and to other people.

There are those who actively seek opportunities to react. Many men wait for a woman to say something so they can immediately respond. They think this gives them points for being witty or quick, but in truth, it only makes the woman feel like the man is a walking reflex, not in control of his responses—she is the one controlling him. Such a man will immediately be assigned low social value.

These men are also prone to extreme emotional reactions. You can often see them reacting dramatically to what a woman says.

On the other hand, there are people who do not seek opportunities to react. They do not "jump" at every external stimulus to deal with it. They are capable of staying calm and are less influenced by their surroundings. They are less prone to extreme emotions like anger or laughter as a response. When a woman says something to them, they can continue acting as if nothing happened. Their facial expressions don't change—they remain unaffected. They might respond verbally, but their internal state remains unchanged. They don't become happier, angrier, or sadder—they are not emotionally affected at all. These are the men who receive high value because of their behavior.

To gain higher value, you need to have a stable internal state, unaffected by others' actions.

We value people when we feel we cannot influence them. To achieve higher value, you don't need to emotionally influence someone else. It's enough to be stable in your position.

Simply not being emotionally affected when someone else tries to influence you will trigger an emotional response in the other person. When people see that the emotional reaction they expected from you doesn't come, it immediately challenges them. When you remain unaffected in situations where others expect you to react, you automatically place yourself in a different position from most people, and your value increases.

The Key Is Not Indifference

The secret isn't about being indifferent; it's about maintaining a steady internal state in response to external stimuli. Nothing external shakes you; your emotions aren't controlled by the actions and words of others. Your internal state changes only when you decide, not as a reaction to external stimuli.

When a woman says something to you, you don't need to act "cool," but you do need to maintain the same internal state you had before she spoke. If you were laughing, your internal state shouldn't break because of what she said—you keep laughing. She didn't cause any change in your internal state.

Starting now, begin observing yourself and identifying automatic reactions that arise when you communicate with a woman. These could be smiles, extra attention when you hear her voice, or any other reaction that changes your internal state and that she can notice. Once you identify these things and become aware of them, you can eliminate them by simply stopping. Practice maintaining zero internal change when communicating with a woman. No matter what she says, nothing inside you changes, and you express no emotional shift. She can't influence you, but she can be influenced by you.

Remember: We gain high value when we position ourselves as the "more important" person.

Seizing the Opportunity - Making the Most of Every Situation

Once upon a time, there were two tigers.

One circled around its prey, afraid to scare it away. Eventually, it died of hunger.

The other tiger saw the prey and immediately leaped at it with all its strength!

The prey was a juicy antelope.

An old Russian fable.

A successful man is one who moves towards the events in his life instead of waiting for them to come to him.

You could be a man with the most wonderful qualities—interesting, educated, understanding, captivating, loving. But if you do nothing, sit at home, or linger in the darkest corner of the local pub waiting for something to happen on its own, you'll be in for a disappointment.

Only you can be responsible for everything that happens in your life, and for things to happen, you must take initiative and act in every possible situation. You are the only one who must push the situation to the maximum you can. The responsibility is always on you. Things don't just happen on their own.

There are countless opportunities around you, and if you don't use them, they'll disappear forever. When you see a woman you find attractive, think the following: "I can approach her, get to know her, and this could be the beginning of an extraordinary adventure. If I do nothing now, I will deprive myself of the pleasure of getting to know her, the fun I could have with her, and maybe in a few minutes, someone else will approach her, meet her, and enjoy what I missed out on."

If you want to succeed, you need to take the initiative and act in the best way you can at this moment.

When you're in a club and see a woman you find attractive, you can either approach her or not. But if you don't approach her now, someone else will, and they'll enjoy the experience that you could have had just moments ago.

Understand that every moment you do not take the initiative, you are missing out on the fun, enjoyment, and happiness you could get from the women there. If you don't seize the opportunities, someone else will, and they'll get all the joy you could have had. It's time to take control of your life and start steering it in the direction you want.

Let's refine the translation together

I've reviewed your text and have a few suggestions to enhance the translation. Here's a revised version, focusing on clarity, natural language, and maintaining the original intent:

Conquering the Hard-to-Get Woman

Women desire to be loved, to be conquered by a man, and to be seduced. This desire is deeply rooted in our genes, dating back to the time of primitive man. While every woman wants to be conquered, almost none wants to appear easy.

How does this manifest? One step closer to intimacy, and she resists. She says, "No way," sending the message, "I can't do that so quickly." Or, "I can't be so easy." So how do you overcome her red lines in a particular situation? A woman is afraid to deal with emotions that may arise as a result of any of her actions. She also feels responsible for how she will feel, and therefore decides what to allow and what not to.

To lead a woman to the point the man wants to lead her to, he must remove from her the responsibility for how she will feel and take responsibility for what will happen next. He should leave her only with the emotions she is willing and wanting to experience consciously.

A story for example of a guy who successfully completed our course:
Not long ago I met someone for the first time. We met in the park and we were walking, talking, and getting closer to the parking lot. I gently take her by the waist and turn her gently towards my car. She realizes I'm leading her to the car, stops and says to me: "I'm not getting into a car with someone I barely know." I recognize that she didn't expect this, she's a little nervous and doesn't allow herself to take the next step. I ask her: "Where do you need to be and at what time?" She says she needs to be at place X at time Y. I answer her: "You'll be at place X, at time Y, right after that we get in the car and drive."

What happened here? At first, he left her to deal with the fact that she was getting into a car with a guy she had barely seen for two minutes of her life, to drive - it's unclear where. When he saw that she was not ready to take responsibility for what was going to happen, he let her know that:

a. He understands this and he understands her feelings. b. He is willing to take responsibility for what will happen with her in the future. c. He is the one who will make sure she gets to the place she needs to be at the time she needs to be. d. When she had difficulty making a decision, he gave her additional information that helped her make a decision. e. He supported her when she got stuck, and gave her the feeling that he would support her in difficult times in the future.

Women want to be around a man who will take on all the responsibility, and they can trust him with their eyes closed. The message you need to convey to her is that she won't have to worry, that you're taking on all the responsibility for what will happen and that everything will be fine and she'll enjoy it.

And a little more for dessert...

Someone once said: "The winner is the one whose reality is stronger."

Each of you believes in something. You believe you'll sleep with her tonight, and she believes she won't give you today. What will really happen? Whose belief will come true? The belief of the stronger one will come true. The one who is more confident in what will happen, the one who has fewer doubts, the one who doesn't hesitate along the way and thinks less about ways to achieve his goal (because he is sure that, one way or another, this is what will happen), is the one who will dictate reality for both of you.

There is a certain boundary that, when crossed, the woman stops thinking, and you will not encounter the problems presented above. This boundary consists of two main parameters:

a. The level of her interest in you. Once she wants you, you won't encounter obstacles. She will draw you into a stormy sex life without you having time to blink. So know that as soon as you encounter an obstacle, she probably doesn't want you enough yet.

b. Her ability to think. As long as she thinks, you may encounter obstacles. But once their thoughts disconnect, only the basic instincts remain, and I hope you can distinguish between the survival instinct and the reproductive instinct and influence the right one.

These two parameters are very dependent on each other. Once one of them is met, the boundary is crossed, all her defenses fall and you will be the one who has to defend himself :)

How to Schedule a Date Over the Phone and Make It the Date of Your Dreams

Many people get stuck when it comes to setting up a date. They know how to approach, they manage to talk freely, create attraction, and get a phone number, but they freeze when it's time to call and schedule the date.

Let me show you the key steps to effectively scheduling a date, so that women will want to meet you every time you ask.

When to Call?

Some might tell you not to call too soon, because it shows that you have nothing else going on and puts her at the top of your priority list. Others will say not to wait too long, or she might lose interest.

I say, don't stick to any of these rules. They'll only stress you out, and they have no real impact on the effectiveness of your call. Call when it's most convenient for you—when you're in a good mood and genuinely excited about setting up a date with her. What really matters during the call is that you're positive, relaxed, enthusiastic, and make the conversation fun and engaging. These qualities aren't linked to the amount of time that's passed since you got her number; they depend entirely on your personal skills and mood at that moment.

When you got her number, you should have asked her when would be a convenient time to call. Be mindful of this information—you don't want to catch her in the middle of work or in a situation where she can't talk. I recommend calling as soon as possible, even on the same day. Who knows? Tomorrow you might not have the time, or you might want to meet someone new.

My experience, and that of many of our students, shows that calling the same day or even 15 minutes after getting her number yields great results and is often the best recipe for success.

The Essence of the Call: Keep It Short and Schedule the Date

The phone call shouldn't be too long. She's not your best friend who just got back from Australia and you need to catch up with. The goal of the call is to set up a date. You're not her phone buddy, and there's no need for a half-hour heart-to-heart. Just a few minutes is enough to reignite attraction, make her excited to see you, and set a date.

If you're used to having long conversations before the date, you're not being effective. You're not making progress. You're talking to her not to create a female phone friend. Save the deeper connection and stories for the date—that's what the date is for. Don't deprive yourself or her of the fun of having these conversations face-to-face.

How to Set the Date Itself

After a few minutes of conversation, it will be time to set up the date. Don't wait until you run out of things to say and the conversation starts to fizzle out—that's not the right time to schedule a date. It's better to do it at the peak of the conversation. You can even start the call with something like, "Hey, we're meeting tonight at eight, be ready."

You can transition to setting up the date with lines like:

- "It's really nice talking to you, let's meet tonight at nine and continue."
- "Let's save the good stories for our date. I'll pick you up tomorrow at eight."
- "Listen, I'm not a fan of phone chats—they give me radiation. Let's meet up and have fun."

Any line in this style will work well.

You can also tailor the date to your shared interests. If you've gotten to know each other a bit and realized you both like walking in the park, suggest meeting at the park. If you both like noisy pubs, go for that. I recommend a place where you can talk and get to know each other in a relaxed atmosphere.

What If She Doesn't Answer?

If she doesn't answer your call, there's no reason to read into it. You never really know what's going on with her and why she didn't pick up. She might have been busy, her phone might have been on silent, or she could have been in the bathroom. Don't expect her to call you back—few women do. I'm sure even you don't always return missed calls. You probably think, "If it's important, they'll call again." For women, this mindset is even more ingrained, so don't be lazy—call her again.

Call her later or the next day. If you're always calling at the same time and not getting through, try calling at a different time on a different day.

If she doesn't answer, don't leave voicemails or send texts. Don't put the responsibility on her to call you back—that's not her role. Keep her number aside and try again another time.

Don't Settle for Half-Agreements

Women love to offer half-agreements. A half-agreement is like, "Okay, but call me tomorrow afternoon." She gives you hope of meeting up but keeps an escape route. You haven't actually set anything in stone. If you accept a half-agreement, expect to spend the evening alone. If she leaves herself an out, there's a 95% chance she'll take it.

Half-agreement = no agreement. If you haven't locked down a time and place for the date, it's as if you haven't set up anything at all. Half-agreements always lead to problems, and the dates often get canceled. When you decide to meet with her, lock in the day, exact time, and where you're meeting, so you don't have to discuss details again before the date.

Never accept half-agreements. If you can make plans for tomorrow, so can she. There's no reason she should keep you in the dark until the last minute. If she offers a half-agreement, tell her, "I'm making my plans now, and I don't want to be left hanging until the last minute. I guess you wouldn't want that either. Let's set it now." If she still doesn't agree, end the call politely and try again in a few days if you're still interested.

You Are the Leader

It's crucial to emphasize decision-making, both when planning the date and during the date itself. A real man leads his woman, takes responsibility, and makes her feel like a princess who can trust him. You are the one who should decide where to go, how you'll get there, and when you'll meet.

Many men mistakenly think that letting the woman decide everything will make her the happiest. They ask, "What do you feel like doing?" or "Where do you want to go?" or "What's most comfortable for you?" A woman needs a man who makes decisions for her, someone she can lean on and trust—a man who decides for both of them and takes away as much of the burden of decision-making as possible, whether on a date, during the initial meeting, or in a long-term relationship.

This is where you need to step into the role of the decision-maker. Don't worry about the woman—if she's uncomfortable with your decision, she'll let you know. They're very good at that. If she suggests an alternative that sounds good to you, there's no problem agreeing and going with it.

Help Her Choose What to Wear

Before a date, especially a first date, a woman spends a lot of time choosing her outfit and grooming herself. Many women spend hours running back and forth between the mirror and the closet, trying on and changing clothes until they find what feels right for that day. Sometimes they even cancel dates because they don't think they have anything suitable to wear or they don't feel they look their best.

Help your woman decide—give her a hint about what you'd like her to wear for your date. This will make her life much easier.

Hints could be worked into the conversation, such as, "So wear jeans and a t-shirt—it's going to be a nice day," or "We're going to a club, dress accordingly," or "You're coming in an evening dress, right? It's a fancy event." Any idea along these lines will do the trick. There may be women who think to themselves, "Who is he to tell me what to wear?" but don't worry—that's okay. When they're standing in front of the wardrobe, they'll be grateful for your suggestion.

Secrets of the First Kiss

When you're on a date with a woman, at some point, thoughts about the first kiss will start running through your head. You might think, "When should I kiss her?", "Does she want to kiss me?", "How will she react?", and "Is this the right time?" These questions and concerns can be overwhelming, and the way a man handles the first kiss can determine whether the relationship continues.

Before you kiss her, make sure there is some physical contact between you. Many men make the common mistake of not touching the woman throughout the entire date. Then, when they decide it's time for a kiss, the transition from no contact to a kiss can be too big of a leap for her. This situation can be intimidating, and in most cases, you'll face resistance. If she's not used to your touch, starting to touch her just before the kiss can be too sudden. Once she has become comfortable with your touch and has gotten used to your presence and warmth, it's the right time to move in for the kiss.

When to Kiss?

In all the Hollywood movies, we see the man waiting until the very end, walking the woman to her door, and only then kissing her. Of course, in the movie, everything goes smoothly, and they live happily ever after. But in real life, it doesn't always work like that.

Most men try to mimic this Hollywood scene, kissing at the end of the date when everyone knows it's coming. It's not interesting or exciting. The kiss should happen at the most surprising and unexpected moment—like in the middle of the date. Women remember kisses that come as a surprise.

When you're on a date, you're probably talking, having fun, and maybe even having a drink. You're touching her, enjoying each other's company, and then the thought crosses your mind: "I want to kiss her." That's exactly when you should do it. Most men start making excuses to themselves—"Not now, I'll wait until the end of the evening," or "Maybe she's not ready yet," and many other excuses. Some even wait for a sign from above. They think something has to happen to signal that now is the time.

When you're on a date, and the thought of kissing her comes to mind, that's precisely the right moment to do it.

Put the Talking Aside

I've seen men who, instead of kissing the woman, start talking about it—a kind of attempt to get her permission or to make sure she's ready. Israelis have a reputation for "talking more in bed than actually doing," and it extends to kissing as well. There's no need to talk about the kiss. There's no need to ask, "What do you like?" or "How do you like it?", or the worst question of all: "Can I kiss you?" Not only does this show insecurity, but it also ruins the moment and annoys the woman.

The moral is simple—kiss her when you feel like it, without unnecessary questions.

You may get a "no" the first time you try to kiss her, or she may give you an excuse like, "We don't know each other well enough yet" or "What, so soon?" These are tests women use to check your confidence. Will you fold after the first "no" and go home with your tail between your legs, or will you handle the challenge, give a meaningful response, and move forward?

If you encounter a "no," that's perfectly fine. Continue the conversation, do what you were doing before you tried to kiss her, and after ten minutes, try to kiss her again. After one or two attempts like this, you're guaranteed a kiss, and you'll have proven to her that you are a man who knows how to pursue a woman. If she wasn't ready to kiss you at all, she wouldn't still be on the date with you.

Turn Friendships into Relationships

We all have female friends—some of whom we might want to turn into something casual or even a serious relationship, while others will always remain friends. Throughout a man's life, he often faces the choice of whether to stay in the friend zone, hoping for something to develop in the future, or to take a risk, make a move, and perhaps win the girl.

I'll talk to you about two different situations:

Scenario I - A long-term friendship that you want to change.

Scenario II - A new acquaintance. You've just met, and you're walking a fine line—early meetings will determine whether this will turn into a friendship or something more.

Scenario I - Long-term Friendship

Take a look around you, at the women in your life, at your friends. It could be that the woman you want to turn into something more serious has been attracted to you for a long time, wants you, and you just haven't noticed. In such a case, you need to identify the signs and recognize her interest in you. It's crucial to understand that when a woman is in any type of relationship with you—whether it's friendship or something serious—she chooses to be there and is gaining something from it. Maybe she's wanted you all along; it's up to you to notice, advance, and take action.

What's challenging about leaving the "friend zone" is the behavior patterns of being a "friend" that we've become accustomed to with that specific woman.

It's very uncomfortable to break the status quo, to stop treating a woman the way you've always treated her and start interacting with her differently. If you want to change the situation, leave the friend zone, and make her attracted to you sexually, different behavior must take place.

First, you need to understand what "friend" actions you are doing and stop doing them. Here are a few examples:

- Letting her talk to you about other men and her day-to-day problems.
- Helping her with schoolwork, running errands, or shopping together.
- Having long phone conversations with her, engaging in deep discussions.
- Going out with her regularly as if you're on a date.
- Treating her like one of your male friends.
- Pouring your heart out to her without holding back.
- Letting her test you and asking her for advice.
- Allowing her to oppose you in certain ways.
- Avoiding physical contact, keeping everything at a level of friendly hugs or handshakes.

You introduce her to others as a friend. The status of being "just friends" can only be defined by what you do or don't do together. A partner or lover does different things, and that's why they have a different title. To change roles and become someone other than just a friend, you need to start doing new things. Here are some examples:

- Playing hot and cold.
- Evaluating her and giving her ratings.
- Flirting.
- Physical intimacy.
- Touching and caressing.
- Kissing.
- Sex.

If you decide to leave the friend zone, you have to stop being her best friend. Let her understand that she will never have you in that role again. As long as you continue behaving the way you have until now, you won't be able to change the situation, and you'll waste your energy for nothing.

The best approach is to disappear for a long period, cutting all contact—ideally for at least six months. When you reappear, you'll be in a new role with new behavior patterns. You'll look at her differently, behave differently, and not allow her to reestablish the old dynamic. She must accept the "new you"—someone who interacts with women differently—or not accept you at all. You must know how to make her attracted to you and interested in you. This time, you'll start your relationship on a completely different track, just as you would with someone new.

Another way is to make gradual changes. This method is more difficult because each time you do something new towards her or stop doing something you used to do, she will try to "bring you back" to your old ways. She will want you to behave as you always did and might reject your sudden new behavior. This way presents challenges and requires a lot of patience and effort.

Scenario II – A New Acquaintance

In this situation, you're at a crossroads. The nature of your relationship is still undefined, and it's unclear where it's heading. This is a typical scenario that happens when you meet someone new, often in a social setting, and you have to decide how to establish your relationship—either as a friend or as someone who wants to conquer her heart.

Think, for example, of a time when you went to a party with friends and met someone new—a friend of a friend. What did you decide to do at that moment? Did you immediately make her just another one of your friends, or did you decide that you wanted her and began moving in the right direction?

To avoid ending up in the friend zone, simply avoid doing things that friends do. Use the list from the previous section as a guide. Watch how her other friends behave with her, and don't do any of those things. Even if it limits the amount of communication between you, it's better to have short interactions that create attraction and make it clear there's no chance of being just friends. She needs to clearly understand that you're not someone who can fill the role of a friend. With you, it's either intimate/romantic or nothing.

It's crucial to remember: If you have to choose between friendship with her or nothing, you must choose nothing! As long as you keep the idea of friendship as an option in your mind, you're likely to end up there. Erase that option entirely, and don't let it happen.

What to Do When She Says, "But We're Just Friends"

You're together, and you've started getting closer on an intimate level. For example, let's say you kissed her on the lips, and afterward, she said, "But we're just friends." This is a sign that either attraction is lacking, or she has a certain fear that you need to address. For instance, she might be afraid of coming across as "easy," and therefore doesn't want to get into something that could make her feel that way.

Never try to convince her that you're "not just friends." Take it as a rule—never try to convince a woman! Instead, reassure her, say, "Of course, we're just friends," and continue what you were doing—keep kissing her. She needs to understand that being "just friends" is no longer an option, even if it was in the past.

When she realizes that friendship is no longer possible and she doesn't want you in a romantic sense, she won't stay around because she knows that you'll never go back to being her friend. If she still stays, it's a sign that you can continue to move forward confidently.

Every Friend Has Friends

If, in the end, you don't succeed or choose to keep her as a friend, remember that every friend has plenty of friends. Use your friendships wisely—each of your friends can introduce and recommend you to her friends, opening new opportunities in your life. After all, friends help each other out, and as a guy, you need someone. Who better to help you than your good friend? ⬚

A Story of Success

Let me share a story from one of my friends about how he slept with someone he was friends with before.

Oliver's Story:

I met this girl, and we were just friends—nothing more than the usual friendship I have with anyone. So yesterday, we talked.

Attraction:

She said: "It's so annoying to be home alone."

I replied: "Got the hint, I'll see if I'm free and come over."

She was shocked and laughed for what seemed like an hour!

Later in the evening, I called her and we talked for about 20 minutes.

I said: "Hey, blah blah blah."

She said: (in the middle of the conversation) "I just remembered how we met."

I realized this was my chance: "I'll come over at 11 after my workout."

She said: "No, what are you talking about."

I said: "Don't worry, we won't have sex, we'll just talk."

She was shocked, hesitated, and stammered: "N-no..."

I asked: "Do you have a bathtub?"

She said: "Yes, why?"

I said: "Because I've never taken a bath in my life (true story)."

She got excited about the idea and started talking about what she puts in the water and all that (and the conversation flowed again).

I said: "Anyway, I'll be there at 11."

She said: "No, that's not okay."

I said: "I'll just take a bath and go to sleep, no sex, so don't get your hopes up." She laughed and agreed.

At 11, she met me downstairs. I went up to her room and started getting comfortable—talking about her books, the TV, wandering around her place like I was buying it. Then I went to the bath, and she prepared an amazing one for me (I sat in there for two hours).

I got out of the bath, and we went to bed. After five minutes of lying down, I started play-fighting with her.

I said: (pushing her off the bed and shouting) "This is my bed! You have enough space on the carpet."

She said: "What a jerk, I've never heard anything like this before" (and jumped on me).

We started play-fighting, which then turned into intense make-out sessions. Slowly, after about four hours of fooling around, we finally had sex.

Approach:

Full of hope—zero expectations.

What I Learned:

- "No" is like a stop sign—it means you need to take a step back and then continue moving forward.
    - (For example, I kissed her ear, then her neck. When I moved to her chest, she stopped me. So, I went back to her neck, then to her chest again, and this time she didn't say "no." She must have said "stop" at least 500 times, but each time I just adjusted.)
- Don't talk while making out.
- Be consistent!

At the end, I was lying on my back, and she was lying with her body open towards me, stroking my chest. I started asking her some questions that might interest you too.

I asked: "Is it true that all girls do it?"

She said: "Yeah, in the shower... You have no idea how many of your female friends do it." (I was shocked for a few minutes).

I said: "You told me 'no' like 500 times, and yet here you are, naked next to me."

She said: "I don't know, it's like a reflex, maybe because I'm testing how persistent you are."

I asked: "By the way, what kind of guys are girls attracted to? Do you know?"

She said: "There's no fixed model."

I said: "But if there is one, what would he be like?"

She said: "Someone real, not someone putting on a show or flaunting his money."

I asked: "And you don't care if he has a small dick?"

She said: "Oh, come on, who cares about that."

Learn to Ask the Right Questions in a Conversation

It's well known that men often complicate themselves by asking the wrong questions and not knowing how to steer the conversation to the desired point. Here, we'll go over some techniques you can use to make the conversation more interesting for both her and you.

Open and Closed Questions

Most men tend to "kill" their conversation with a woman by asking closed questions. Closed questions are those that have short and definitive answers. Such questions typically have only a limited number of possible responses. Questions like, "Do you like animals?", "Where do you work?", or "Are you a vegetarian?" fall into this category. In closed questions, it's hard for the woman to express herself and develop the topic. Many men tend to ask questions like, "Did you like the movie we watched?", where the possible answers are "yes" or "no", instead of asking questions that allow for an open response, such as "What scenes did you like most in the movie? Why those specifically?" or "How do you think the ending could have been improved?" Closed questions are the exact kind of questions that make a conversation feel like a job interview.

Open questions are those where the answer is not implied by the question. Just like the earlier example of questions about the movie. With open questions, the woman has a chance to be creative, connect to her emotions, develop the topic, and keep the conversation flowing much better. From her answer to an open question, many new ideas and interesting subjects to talk about can arise.

When you're with a woman, try to use as many open questions as possible and let her connect to her feelings and express them. Emotions in conversation are one of the most important things for her.

There are men who claim that women don't engage with them during a conversation when all they ask are questions like "Where are you from?", "What are you studying?" Questions like these have prepared answers, and she doesn't need to think much about how to respond. In the end, she comes across as dull and boring only because the man directed her to an answer that made it hard for the conversation to develop.

A man who asks closed questions is conducting a job interview instead of having a fun conversation with her, so it's no wonder she doesn't enjoy it or engage.

Question Leap

The question leap is a powerful technique that allows you to move the conversation and the situation a step forward. Men who use this technique face very few obstacles and achieve their goals quickly. The question leap technique is very simple. All you need to do is skip one question ahead. For example, instead of asking, "Do you want to go out today?", you ask, "Should I pick you up at eight or nine?" Here, we skipped over the question of whether she wants to go out and assumed the answer is "yes."

Instead of asking, "Do you want a drink?", you ask, "Should I get you wine or a cocktail?"

Instead of asking, "Can I get your phone number?", you ask, "When would you be free to chat on the phone?"

The question leap is excellent for moving forward in the conversation because, in this situation, you are assuming that the woman has already answered "yes" to the question you skipped, and you can proceed to the next question. When you leap forward, you dictate the conversation, and you've essentially already dictated the "yes" that she supposedly gave earlier—now all that's left is to keep progressing.

Directed Question

Men tend to sabotage their relationships and dates by using questions that work against them. When you ask someone a question, they immediately start thinking about the topic to be able to answer. Try to think if you've ever asked a woman, "Are you mad at me?" What happens at that moment is that she starts considering whether she's actually mad at you and tries to measure what it's like to be angry with you. If you ask her, "Are you mad at me?", chances are you noticed something, so she'll start looking for it! The worst part is if she replies, "No, not at all..." and then you keep insisting, "No, I can see you're mad at me..." This action will only cause her to find reasons—reasons that might not even exist—to justify why she is mad at you.

So next time you're thinking of asking such questions, think twice about what image you're creating in her mind and what options you're opening up for her to consider as possibilities when you ask.

Directed questions can also be used to your advantage by asking questions like, "Are you attracted to me?", "Why are you acting like you're falling for me?" and similar things. Even if it sounds a bit strange at first, it works, and she will start building in her mind the image you led her to imagine.

The Deadly Silence – A Powerful Tool for Creating Interest and Attraction

I've come to the conclusion that the thing that will set you apart (at least from me) from anyone else going on a date with a woman isn't how many routines you run on her, or how witty, edgy, or interesting you are. All of that is important, but it won't necessarily take you out of the "funny and witty guy" box, which is a category that a lot of guys fall into. I've heard of many guys who went out with a girl, performed well, did everything right, got the feedback they wanted, but in the end, everything fizzled out. It was as if what they did lacked the depth needed to truly get under her skin. Everything was good but stayed on the surface.

In my opinion, it's because many don't put enough emphasis on silence.

Silence does four main things:

1. **Shows You're Confident**: It shows you're confident and don't feel the need to keep the conversation going non-stop. You don't feel the need to prove anything to her or anyone else. This is, so far, the strongest tool I've seen (yes, I'm still learning) for showing that you simply don't care what she thinks about you. Sometimes someone who stays silent can come across as having lower value than someone who talks nonsense, but if you can manage to stay silent and still project confidence and comfort, it has a huge impact.
2. **Makes Her Work for the Conversation**: It makes the woman put in the effort to carry the conversation—she's now chasing your cooperation instead of just sitting back and laughing at yet another tired routine. You are the prize.
3. **Brings Out Interesting Things from Her**: It gives her time to think, to digest everything that's happened so far on the date. At least from my relatively limited experience, this is always a good thing.
4. **Makes You Mysterious**: Silence creates mystery. It's not the norm. Someone who knows how to talk, who has been flowing with the conversation up until now, suddenly goes quiet. It makes her think, "What's going on with this guy, what's on his mind?" I've heard phrases like, "Your silence intrigues me." It creates great interest and curiosity.

Of course, silence is a dangerous tool because:

1. **It's Effective Only After You've Proven Yourself**: It's only effective after the woman has seen that you know what you're doing, and when you talk, you know how to say the right things. If you just stay silent without first establishing yourself as someone who knows how to talk, you'll just come off as weird. The idea is to convey that you "know what to say, have something to say, but choose to stay silent."
2. **If You Mess Up, You're in Trouble**: Everything can be fixed, but if you stay silent, and when the silence breaks you project insecurity or discomfort, it sends a very negative message that will require a lot of work to fix. You need to be extremely confident in everything you're conveying (body language, speech, eye contact, etc.) during the silence and afterward.

This is a very powerful thing that I think can distinguish between many good pick-up artists and a great one. Sit the same woman down with five different guys, and I bet she'll choose the one who also knows how to stay silent.

That's it. This came to me after talking with a woman I've been in a sort-of romantic relationship with for a while, and for most of the conversation, I stayed silent. But when I did speak, I said good things that made her laugh. When she asked why I was so quiet, I confidently answered, "I like to stay silent sometimes, it's a way of seeing what will come out of you in such a situation." It worked great and made her feel like she was being tested the whole time.

Progression Stages from Meeting to Sex

If we look at the entire process from meeting to sex, we can divide it into several stages—introduction, post-introduction date, intimate closeness, and sex. Each of these stages has a beginning and an end. To move through each stage, you need to understand the essence of that stage and focus on what's important to progress. Each stage has its core purpose, and everything else is secondary.

Lately, I've received a lot of messages from people who get stuck in a certain stage because instead of focusing on what's important, they focus on irrelevant aspects. As a result, they end up stuck without making progress. What's even worse is they drag others into discussions about trivialities, missing the main point of that stage. This is why I want to clarify things and briefly explain what happens in the first two stages—the introduction and the date. What's important, what's secondary, and what you should focus on in each of them.

Focus for All Stages

- Enjoy the process!
- Never engage with a woman if you don't enjoy your time with her. It simply won't work.

Introduction Stage

In this stage, your goal is to let the woman understand that there is a guy called *you* who interests her and attracts her.

Here, tests and power struggles appear to determine who is in control—you or her. If you manage to handle these situations well, she will be attracted to you.

Focus in the Introduction Stage: Creating attraction.

Important Points

1. Understand that everything has the right dosage, whether it's teasing, being bold, or being a gentleman. If you find the right balance for the specific woman, she's yours.
2. Many men create attraction; the woman already wants them and hints in every possible way that she wants to take things further beyond the initial conversation. But they keep trying to create more attraction. The woman loses interest because she sees there is no progression, and eventually, she brushes them off. There's no need to keep creating attraction once it's already there to a sufficient level.

Each of the following signs indicates that you've done this stage well, and you can move on to the next:

- You find yourself at the next stage, spending the next hour with her.
- You got her phone number.
- You set a meeting with her.
- She's showing a lot of interest in you, asking direct questions about you.

Post-Introduction Date Stage

This stage can begin a few days or just a few minutes after you've met. If you've moved on to this stage, it means she's interested in you and attracted to you. I hope you understand that if she's attracted, there's no need to keep focusing on creating attraction.

The focus on attraction decreases as the main subject. What remains is to maintain the attraction already created. Simply put, just because she has decided to spend time with you doesn't mean you should turn into her puppy.

In this stage, your goal is to move toward the status of boyfriend, casual partner, or lover—but not a friend. She needs to clearly understand that you're not there to be her friend. Once she gets that, you'll never end up in the friend zone. You'll either be what you want to be, or there'll be nothing.

The Principle of Friendship with a Woman

A woman will not stay connected to you if she wants you just as a friend but understands that you will never fit that role.

Focus in the Date Stage: Progress towards actions of a boyfriend/casual partner/lover. Progress, progress, and progress beyond talk and platonic relationships.

All you need to do here is ask yourself, "What's the next action I need to take to move one step closer to sex?" and do it. This doesn't mean you have to sleep with her in this stage, but it does mean it's time to move forward and not stand still. For the sake of clarity, here's a small list of reasonable actions, roughly in order: touch, kissing, making out, undressing some clothing, oral sex, sex.

To avoid becoming just a friend, you need to take actions that are "not friendly." Someone who takes "non-friend" actions can only be "not a friend."

Note, there's no mention anywhere of creating attraction or figuring out her intentions towards you.

She's already with you; she knows very well why she's with you, and if it doesn't suit her, believe me, she won't waste a second of her life on you. In this regard, it turns out that women have much more courage than men. If it doesn't work for them, they cut it off without guilt.

Key Points and Interim Tasks:

1. **Enjoy the Process** - Do everything in a way that's fun for you. Don't limit yourself to reach success.
2. **Neutralize Her Fears** - Observe what's holding her back and help her overcome it.
3. **Take Full Responsibility** - Don't burden her with logistical questions or choices. Make all decisions yourself and act accordingly. Let her feel that you're handling everything, and everything will be great.
4. **Act, Don't Talk About Acting** - If you want to do something, do it. Don't prepare her verbally for it. There's no need to explain that you're about to kiss her before you do it.

Signs to Progress Further:

1. If you catch yourself, even for a second, hesitating to do something (fearing to fail in advancing), it's a sign that the action you're afraid to take is the most correct thing to do at that moment. Always do what you're most afraid to do now.
2. If she hasn't said "no" to you a few times during your progression, you're either not progressing at all or moving at a very, very slow pace. You might be holding yourself back. If she hasn't said "no," it means you haven't progressed when you could have. She was ready for progression much earlier than you were. She gave you the opportunity, but you didn't take it.

A woman must say "no" a few times before saying "yes." That's perfectly fine. Accept her "no," wait a while, and then move forward again.

She has to say "no" at least to avoid feeling easy. It's a matter of feminine ego. If she said "no" once or more, she knows she resisted a little and agreed to proceed only after her objections—that she didn't just "open her legs" at the first opportunity. This knowledge makes her feel good.

Signs You've Successfully Completed the Stage:

- You find yourself with her at one of your homes.
- You've reached intimate actions (kissing, making out, sex).
- You've arranged to meet at one of your homes.

To conclude, always look at what stage you're at and what's important to do in that stage. Should you still be playing games, creating attraction, teasing her, or is it time to reduce that and start moving forward?

Most failures by men are due to a lack of understanding the right balance and timing. Progressing too quickly, too early, or failing to progress at all and getting stuck in the attraction stage when all signs say to move forward—these are mistakes you need to avoid.

How to Integrate All the Principles from This Book into Your Life

In this book, you've read a lot of information that it's now time to start applying in your life. Your ability to integrate this knowledge and use it effectively will improve more and more if you follow these two rules:

A. Practice. Nothing will start working if you don't practice and repeat it many times. Try out everything you read in the book in the real world. Don't dismiss anything just because it might not make sense to you. If it all made perfect sense to you, you wouldn't need to read this book, and you would've already been doing it. The goal of this book is to show you new things and get you to try them.

B. Self-Feedback. Analyze every interaction with women *only after the fact*. Remember, during the action itself, you must not overthink or analyze. It's likely that while you're with a woman, you won't remember everything you've read here and won't be able to instantly use all the knowledge you've gained. So, when you get home, sit down with yourself and think about how you could have used the principles from this book in the situation you were involved in. What did you forget, and how could you apply it next time? Pat yourself on the back for the things you did well and reinforce them. You can always go back and do again what already works for you, whether it's a successful line, a behavior pattern, or a reaction that gave you good results. If something didn't go well, think about how you could behave differently next time you're in a similar situation, say something else, and achieve a different outcome.

Creating a Supportive Environment – The People Who Will Propel You to Success

Let's talk about the environment we live in and how it affects our progress and successes. When does it propel us forward, and when does it hold us back? Every man has his family circle and his circle of friends. Men who succeed in the world of dating and seduction know how to create a supportive environment that promotes and encourages them to succeed in this area.

For the sake of clarity, let's divide your environment into three circles:

First Circle – The innermost circle. This is you, with all your ideas and goals.

Second Circle – The surrounding circle that includes your family and close friends. This is essentially your immediate environment, the people you see daily—your supportive environment.

Third Circle – The outermost circle that encompasses the previous two. This is your broader external environment—the people you haven't met yet and those you may never meet. This circle also includes the women you want to meet but haven't met yet.

In the world of dating and seduction, some men succeed more than others. Very few men have achieved significant success with women entirely on their own. If you ask a successful man what helped him reach his success, he'll tell you that it was learning through experience and having a supportive environment that encouraged him to continue on this path.

The supportive environment of these successful men may include their family or close friends, who together learned the field, encouraged each other, and conquered the world of women.

I've explained earlier that new women—the ones you want to meet—are in the third circle, the circle of people you haven't met yet. To bring these women closer to your first circle—to bring them to you—they first need to enter the second circle, becoming people you know, like your friends.

Friends Who Don't Support You

Have you ever thought about what happens when your second circle—your friends—are negative about women and don't understand what's going on in this area? When they feel threatened by the entire situation, and instead of helping and supporting you, they hold you back?

Imagine going out to a club or a nice pub with a friend or group of friends, sitting down, and ordering a beer as usual. Suddenly, you notice two beautiful women sitting at the table next to you. You, knowing what you're doing, approach and talk to them. You use the tools to create attraction that you learned from the book or a course. The women laugh and seem interested in you, and you invite them to join your table.

The women happily sit with you, but this is exactly when the problems start. Your friend, feeling helpless in the situation, tries too hard to impress and get out of it, which the women sense, and it doesn't take long for them to leave. Afterward, your friend will make sure to explain why what happened wasn't right. The next time you want to approach new women, he'll try to talk you out of it. He doesn't do this to harm you intentionally—it's just his perception and way of seeing things. He doesn't know any different.

In most cases, no one even approaches or talks to new women, simply because it's not accepted in your circle, and of course, you don't want to stand out as different. Your immediate environment always tries to keep you as you were in the past.

Creating a Supportive Environment for Yourself

It's very important to create a supportive environment for yourself, one that will help you advance in the field and allow you to bring the women you want closer to you safely. You won't believe how much power you can have in a supportive environment. It's no coincidence that successful men hang out together.

To create a supportive environment for yourself, I recommend doing the following:

A. Recommend This Book to Your Friends and Let Them Read It.

You're always welcome to share the information with your friends; don't keep all the fun to yourself. If you think about it, it's every man's dream.

Printed in Great Britain
by Amazon

12100337-529b-4c29-b45c-fa0f434d6157R01